Andrew Mckie, Barrister at Clerksroom Manchester, is a specialist in claimant and defendant personal injury, with a particular interest in cases involving alleged fraud, credit hire, highways, occupiers and defective premises cases. He was previously Head of Litigation and In-House Solicitor Advocate at a claimant personal injury firm with over 50 staff.

Occupiers, Highways and Defective Premises Claims: A Practical Guide Post-Jackson

2nd Edition

Occupiers, Highways and Defective Premises Claims: A Practical Guide Post-Jackson
2nd Edition

Andrew Mckie,
Barrister at Law, Clerksroom (Manchester),
LLB Hons, PG DIP and
Former Solicitor Advocate,

Law Brief Publishing

Published 2018 by Law Brief Publishing, an imprint of Law Brief Publishing Ltd
30 The Parks
Minehead
Somerset
TA24 8BT

www.lawbriefpublishing.com

Paperback: 978-1-911035-37-4

PREFACE

It has not been nearly 4 years since the first edition of this book. The law in relation to these claims has remained largely settled but there are some cases of important note since the last edition. The aim of the updated booked is to examine the updated authorities in relation to highways, occupiers and defective premises claims that have taken place over the last 4 years and offer a clear but comprehensive guide to practice points to be taken from those, along with those that form the original text. There is a particular focus in this edition on all the fixed recoverable costs authorities, which can aid practitioners when dealing with these cases.

The fixed costs rules have remained largely the same since the first edition of this book in 2014, and although the small claim track will increase to £2,000 for EL/PL claims likely in April 2019, most EL/PL cases will likely fall outside this bracket, so this will likely remain a dynamic area of practice. The claims will likely be affected by Jackson's further fixed costs changes to be confirmed, which will likely take effect in 2019.

The book has a focus on running highways, occupiers and defectives premises claims in an economical and efficient way post-Jackson, spotting the winners and vetting the losing claims early on.

The book will aim to cover issues in relation to occupiers cases, highways cases, defective premises and nuisance, and in particular focuses on the day-to-day issues in practice one encounters with such cases.

I would encourage the reader to 'dip in and out' of the book as and when required.

I wish to thank Tim Kevan of Law Brief Publishing for providing me with the opportunity to write this book and for the PI Brief Update website for publishing relevant sections.

Andrew Mckie
Personal Injury Barrister
April 2018

CONTENTS

CHAPTER ONE
FIXED RECOVERABLE COSTS, PORTAL COSTS AND POTENTIAL ROUTES OUT OF FIXED COSTS AND THE PORTAL IN HIGHWAYS AND SLIPPING/TRIPPING CLAIMS

The first chapter of this book is dedicated to the starting point for most Highways Act 1980 and public liability claims; the Low Value Portal. Post July 2013, almost all highways slipping and tripping claims will start out in the Low Value Portal, and once they exit the Low Value Portal, will be subject to Fixed Recoverable Costs. This arguably makes the running of these claims for many law firms, with portal or fixed costs, challenging since highways and public liability cases can sometimes be complex in fact, and often can be complex in Law.

The aim of this book is to provide the reader with an armoury for dealing with these cases in an economic and efficient way. Ultimately, if the portal costs and/or fixed costs become uneconomical for personal injury firms to run these cases, firms will cease to undertake this type of work, and access to justice for seriously injured clients will be restricted. The following guidance is a summary of the costs rules for dealing with such claims in the Low Value Portal and the costs that are recoverable when dealing with such claims within Fixed Recoverable Costs (FRCs).

Public Liability and Highways Claims – Fixed Costs – Costs for Claims That Exit The Portal after 31 July 2013 – CPR 45

Fixed costs where a claim no longer continues under the EL/PL Protocol – public liability claims			
A. If Parties reach a settlement prior to the claimant issuing proceedings under Part 7			
Agreed damages	At least £1,000, but not more than £5,000	More than £5,000, but not more than £10,000	More than £10,000, but not more than £25,000
Fixed costs	The total of—(a) £950; and(b) 17.5% of the damages	The total of—(a) £1,855; and(b) 10.5% of damages over £5,000	The total of—(a) £2,370; and(b) 10% of damages over £10,000
B. If proceedings are issued under Part 7, but the case settles before trial			
Stage at which case is settled	On or after the date of issue, but prior to the date of allocation under Part 26	On or after the date of allocation under Part 26, but prior to the date of listing	On or after the date of listing but prior the date of trial
Fixed costs damages	The total of—(a) £2,450; and(b) 17.5% of the damages	The total of—(a) £3,065; and(b) 22.5% of the damages	The total of—(a) £3,790; and(b) 27.5% of the damages

C. If the claim is disposed of at trial			
Fixed costs	The total of—(a) £3,790;(b) 27.5% of the damages agreed or awarded; and (c) the relevant trial advocacy fee		

Which Claims Do The Portals Apply To?

The Pre-Action Protocol for Low Value Personal Injury Public Liability Claims will apply to most public liability claims up to the value of £25,000 in respect of an accident occurring on or after 31 July 2013 or, in a disease claim, where no letter of claim has been sent to the defendant before 31 July 2013.

Public Liability Portal Costs

CPR 45.16 sets out the relevant fees that are recoverable in the Low Value Portal:-

(1)   *This Section applies to claims that have been or should have been started under Part 8 in accordance with Practice Direction 8B ('the Stage 3 Procedure').*

(2)   *Where a party has not complied with the relevant Protocol rule 45.24 will apply.*

       'The relevant Protocol' means

       (b)   the Pre-action Protocol for Low Value Personal Injury Claims (Employers' Liability and Public Liability) Claims ('the EL/PL Protocol)

TABLE 6A

Fixed costs in relation to the EL/PL Protocol			
Where the value of the claim for damages is not more than £10,000	Where the value of the claim for damages is more than £10,000, but not more than £25,000		
Stage 1 fixed costs	£300	Stage 1 fixed costs	£300
Stage 2 fixed costs	£600	Stage 2 fixed costs	£1300
Stage 3- Type A fixed costs	£250	Stage 3- Type A fixed costs	£250
Stage 3- Type B fixed costs	£250	Stage 3- Type B fixed costs	£250
Stage 3- Type C fixed costs	£150	Stage 3- Type C fixed costs	£150

What about public liability portal disbursements?

CPR 45.19 sets out the relevant disbursements recoverable in the PL portal:-

(1)   *The court:-*

   (a) may allow a claim for a disbursement of a type mentioned in paragraphs (2) or (3); but

(b) will not allow a claim for any other type of disbursement.

(2) *In a claim to which either the RTA Protocol or EL/PL Protocol applies, the disbursements referred to in paragraph (1) are:-*

(a) the cost of obtaining –

(i) medical records;

(ii) a medical report or reports or non-medical expert reports as provided for in the relevant Protocol;

(b) court fees as a result of Part 21 being applicable;

(c) court fees payable where proceedings are started as a result of a limitation period that is about to expire;

(d) court fees in respect of the Stage 3 Procedure; and

(e) any other disbursement that has arisen due to a particular feature of the dispute.

Counsel's Advice on Quantum/Liability

Additional advice on the value of the claim

45.23B

Where:-

(a) the value of the claim for damages is more than £10,000;

(b) an additional advice has been obtained from a specialist solicitor or from counsel;

(c) that advice is reasonably required to value the claim,

the fixed costs may include an additional amount equivalent to the Stage 3 Type C fixed costs. **This is £150.**

It is therefore important to note:-

(a)   Counsel's advice on liability/causation **will not be recoverable as a disbursement**, under normal circumstances.

(b)   It will be important to look early to other courses of funding if advice is required on LEI/ATE/BTE cover. An indemnity will be required.

What Disbursements Are Recoverable Under Fixed Recoverable Costs For PL Claims?

45.29I sets out the relevant disbursements that are recoverable under FRCs for claims that start in the portal and then fall out:-

(1) The court:-

(a) may allow a claim for a disbursement of a type mentioned in paragraphs (2) or (3); but

(b) will not allow a claim for any other type of disbursement.

(2) In a claim started under either the RTA Protocol or the EL/PL Protocol, the disbursements referred to in paragraph (1) are:-

(a) the cost of obtaining medical records and expert medical reports as provided for in the relevant Protocol;

(b) the cost of any non-medical expert reports as provided for in the relevant Protocol;

(c) the cost of any advice from a specialist solicitor or counsel as provided for in the relevant Protocol;

(d) court fees;

(e) any expert's fee for attending the trial where the court has given permission for the expert to attend;

(f) expenses which a party or witness has reasonably incurred in travelling to and from a hearing or in staying away from home for the purposes of attending a hearing;

(g) a sum not exceeding the amount specified in Practice Dir ection 45 for any loss of earnings or loss of leave by a party or witness due to attending a hearing or to staying away from home for the purpose of attending a hearing; and

(h) any other disbursement reasonably incurred due to a particular feature of the dispute.

Fixed Costs – is there a way out?

Under 45.29J, the Court can order an amount greater than fixed recoverable costs:-

(1) If it considers that there are __exceptional circumstances making it appropriate to do so,__ the court will consider a claim for an amount of costs (excluding disbursements) which is greater than the fixed recoverable costs referred to in rules 45.29B to 45.29H.

(2) If the court considers such a claim to be appropriate, it may:-

(a) summarily assess the costs; or

(b) make an order for the costs to be subject to detailed assessment.

(3) If the court does not consider the claim to be appropriate, it will make an order:-

(a) if the claim is made by the claimant, for the fixed recoverable costs; or

(b) if the claim is made by the defendant, for a sum which has regard to, but which does not exceed the fixed recoverable costs, and any permitted disbursements only.

However, standard highways and/ or Public Liability cases are unlikely to be exceptional.

CPR 45.29k, sets out what happens if there is a failure to achieve an amount greater than fixed recoverable costs.

Failure to achieve costs greater than fixed recoverable costs

45.29K

(1) This rule applies where:-

(a) costs are assessed in accordance with rule 45.29J(2); and

(b) the court assesses the costs (excluding any VAT) as being an amount which is in a sum less than 20% greater than the amount of the fixed recoverable costs.

(2) The court will make an order for the party who made the claim to be paid the lesser of:-

(a) the fixed recoverable costs; and

(b) the assessed costs.

Conclusions

It is clear that the introduction of Fixed Recoverable Costs will make this work unattractive to some firms. However, if one looks at the fees for progressing such claims to trial, these are still attractive and not hugely disproportionate to the fees that would have been recovered under the pre-Jackson costs regime. CFA uplifts and ATE premiums have now been abolished post April 2013, which means that in a post-Jackson era, the base fee is that all that will be recovered.

However, if firms pick and choose the cases to run to trial carefully and obtain early disclosure from the defendant, it will still be possible to make a reasonable profit on these cases for PI firms and more importantly give clients with serious injuries access to justice. Most PI firms post April 2013 operate a CFA agreement with the lay client where they receive some of the damages under the CFA, and this, combined with fixed recoverable costs, can make these claims economic to run. The aim of the subsequent chapters is to look at the new CPR rules concerning Part 36, interim applications and QOCS post July 2013, to offer practical advice as to how highways and slipping and tripping claims can be vetted, investigated and then issued quickly within fixed costs and under Solicitor Conditional Fee Agreements. It is clear that the pre-Jackson days of running claims to trial in the hope that they may settle are now gone, given that under Fixed Costs, the incentive for the defendant to settle, formerly the CFA uplift have now disappeared for post July 2013 cases. Jackson has changed the litigation landscape but if one adopts suitable litigation tactics, it is still possible to run an efficient firm dealing with highways, slipping and tripping cases. The following chapters will show you how, and with a particular focus on vetting cases at the outset and spotting the winners from the potential losing cases quickly and efficiently. There is still a vibrant market for law firms wishing to undertake these types of cases, and potential opportunities under Jackson for firms to undertake this type of work and deal with it as a specialism.

CHAPTER TWO
PUBLIC LIABILITY AND HIGHWAYS CLAIMS POST-JACKSON: PART 36 AND LITIGATION TACTICS – UPDATED 2018 TO INCLUDE BROADHURST V TAN, CHAPMAN V TAMESIDE HEALTH AUTHORITY, SHARPE V LEEDS CITY COUNCIL AND BIRD V ACORN

It is clear that in post-Jackson, post 31 July 2013 highways and public liability cases, the incentives for defendants and insurers to settle these cases has been substantially reduced. These cases are now subject to portal and fixed recoverable costs, and as we have seen from the previous chapter the insurer can now run three or four of these claims to trial and lose them, for effectively the same costs as running one CFA claim to trial, with a 100% uplift under the pre-Jackson regime and losing that at trial.

This new litigation landscape of course poses enormous difficulties for claimant lawyers. For the '50/50' cases that previously may have been issued and then settled, before trial, this is no longer likely to happen. This means that law firms, more than ever, will have to be careful to vet claims before taking them on. To run a profitable department post-Jackson, the majority of claims will have to succeed, given there is no longer the flexibility of CFA uplifts to cushion the shortfalls of the cases that are lost at trial.

This chapter deals with using the new amendments to the CPR post April 2013 and post July 2013, when the Jackson reforms came into effect to:

- Vet cases early on;
- Obtain disclosure quickly; and

- Settle the case before it gets to trial, using Part 36 to encourage that.

Pre-Action Protocols

If a case exits the Low Value Portal i.e. because liability has not been admitted by the defendant (or for any other reason), then the case will still fall within the personal injury Pre-Action Protocol which says:-

> *"3.7*
> *The **defendant('s insurers) will have a maximum of three months** from the date of acknowledgment of the claim **to investigate**. No later than the end of that period the defendant (insurer) shall reply, stating whether liability is denied and, if so, giving reasons for their denial of liability including any alternative version of events relied upon"*

Further it goes on:-

> *"3.10*
> *If the **defendant denies liability**, he should enclose with the letter of reply, **documents** in his possession which are **material to the issues** between the parties, and which would be likely to be ordered to be disclosed by the court, either on an application for pre-action disclosure, or on disclosure during proceedings.*

> *3.11*
> *Attached at Annex B are **specimen**, but non-exhaustive, **lists** of documents likely to be material in different types of claims. Where the claimant's investigation of the case is well advanced, the letter of claim could indicate which classes of documents are considered relevant for early disclosure. Alternatively these could be identified at a later stage.*

> *3.12*
> *Where the defendant admits primary liability, but alleges contrib-*

utory negligence by the claimant, the defendant should give reasons supporting those allegations and disclose those documents from Annex B which are relevant to the issues in dispute. The claimant should respond to the allegations of contributory negligence before proceedings are issued".

The protocol says that the documents to be disclosed for highway tripping claims are:-

"HIGHWAY TRIPPING CLAIMS

Documents from Highway Authority for a period of 12 months prior to the accident:-
(i) Records of inspection for the relevant stretch of highway.

(ii) Maintenance records including records of independent contractors working in the relevant area.

(iii) Records of the minutes of highway authority meetings where maintenance or repair policy has been discussed or decided.

(iv) Records of complaints about the state of highways.

(v) Records of other accidents which have occurred on the relevant stretch of highway"

For trips or slips in the workplace, the relevant documents are:-

"WORKPLACE CLAIMS

(i) Accident book entry.

(ii) First aider report.

(iii) Surgery record.

(iv) Foreman/supervisor accident report.

(v) Safety representative's accident report.

(vi) RIDDOR (Reporting of Injuries, Diseases and Dangerous Occurrences Regulations) report to HSE.

(vii) Other communications between defendants and HSE.

(viii) Minutes of Health and Safety Committee meeting(s) where accident/matter considered.

(ix) Report to DSS.

(x) Documents listed above relative to any previous accident/matter identified by the claimant and relied upon as proof of negligence.

(xi) Earnings information where defendant is employer.

Documents produced to comply with requirements of the Management of Health and Safety at Work Regulations 1992:-

(i) Pre-accident Risk Assessment required by Regulation 3.

(ii) Post-accident Re-Assessment required by Regulation 3.

(iii) Accident Investigation Report prepared in implementing the requirements of Regulations 4, 6 and 9.

(iv) Health Surveillance Records in appropriate cases required by Regulation 5.

(v) Information provided to employees under Regulation 8.

(vi) Documents relating to the employees' health and safety training required by Regulation 11"

There is no specific protocol for occupiers claims but you are likely to want to ask for the following documents, or indeed in any other slip or trip claim:-

- Cleaning and inspections records including copy of the janitor log.

- The accident report form.

- Photographs of where the accident took place.

- Any CCTV evidence.

- Risk assessments.

- Personnel records.

- Previous accidents at the same location for 12 months pre and post-accident.

- Records of previous complaints for 12 months pre and post-accident.

- Measurements of any defect with photographs.

- Previous complaints of the same defect.

- Maintenance records.

- Staff training records.

- Supervisor records and records of any supervisor checks.

It is advisable that the letter requesting the disclosure is sent as soon as the case exits the portal, then a further request is made 14 days before the end of the protocol period and a final request at the end of the protocol period. Each request should say that if the **full** documents are not disclosed, an application will be made for pre-action disclosure at the end of the protocol period, and the costs sought of the application, without any further recourse or warning. This will give the defendant plenty of notice of the application and should give the claimant some chance of recovering the costs of the application at the hearing. It should be borne in mind that on a PAD application, the general rule is that the party making the disclosure gets the costs of the application unless there has been some unreasonable conduct in responding to the disclosure requests. This is why these letters are important in terms of the costs of the application, as they will seek to displace the costs provisions at any subsequent hearing.

If the defendant contends it does not hold a document, it should be asked to sign a disclosure statement, with an appropriate statement of truth, to say the document is not available.

The Pre-Action Disclosure Application

It is arguable that pre action disclosure applications are one of the most common applications in personal injury litigation. Unlike a road traffic claim, the defendant's disclosure is almost always required to assess a section 58 defence in a highways claim or for example, the cleaning and inspection regime in a supermarket slip and trip case.

The CPR sets out:-

Disclosure before proceedings start

> "31.16
>
> (1) This rule applies where an application is made to the court under any Act for disclosure before proceedings have started1.
>
> (2) The application must be supported by evidence.
>
> (3) The court may make an order under this rule only where:-

(a) the respondent is likely to be a party to subsequent proceedings;

(b) the applicant is also likely to be a party to those proceedings;

(c) if proceedings have started, the respondent's duty by way of standard disclosure, set out in rule 31.6, would extend to the documents or classes of documents of which the applicant seeks disclosure; and

(d) disclosure before proceedings have started is desirable in order to:-

> *(i) dispose fairly of the anticipated proceedings;*

> *(ii) assist the dispute to be resolved without proceedings; or*

> *(iii) save costs.*

(4) An order under this rule must:-

> *(a) specify the documents or the classes of documents which the respondent must disclose; and*

> *(b) require him, when making disclosure, to specify any of those documents:-*

>> *(i) which are no longer in his control; or*

>> *(ii) in respect of which he claims a right or duty to withhold inspection.*

(5) Such an order may:-

> *(a) require the respondent to indicate what has happened to any documents which are no longer in his*

control; and

(b) specify the time and place for disclosure and inspection".

It is arguable that as soon as the case reaches the end of the protocol period, if full disclosure has not been provided to enable the claimant's lawyer to assess the claim, an application should be made immediately given a) the claimant's lawyer within fixed costs needs the documents to assess the prospects of success, b) a decision cannot be reached without those documents, and c) the pre action protocols (in most scenarios) are very specific as to what should be disclosed pre-issue.

In making the application it is important that the application sets out in detail, a) what the accident circumstances are, b) the nature of the claimant's investigations, c) what response the defendant has made to the request, and d) most importantly, why each of the documents are required.

The majority of PAD applications, in the author's experience, settle before they ever get to a hearing, but it is clear post-Jackson, it is more important than ever that disclosure is given in full and on time, so claimant lawyers can make quick and efficient decisions, about which cases are to be closed and the ones that are to be litigated. It must be the case, that with FRCs it will no longer be efficient to chase defendants for documents for months or even years, and for cases which are likely to have less than 50% prospects to be sat in claimant lawyer's cabinets waiting for disclosure to come in order to assess them.

Part 36 – Making the Defendant Settle, Once Out Of The Low Value Portal For Post 31 July 2013 Cases

Post-Jackson, one of the only ways that the Defendant may be encouraged to settle a highways slipping and tripping claim, or any other claim for that matter, that stays within fixed costs may be by way of the new Part 36 rules, which came into effect in July 2013. These are set out below as follows:-

Costs consequences following judgment: Trial/Disposal

36.14

(1) Subject to rule 36.14A, this rule applies whereupon judgment being entered:-

(b) judgment against the defendant is at least as advantageous to the claimant as the proposals contained in a claimant's Part 36 offer.

(1A) For the purposes of paragraph (1), in relation to any money claim or money element of a claim, 'more advantageous' means better in money terms by any amount, however small, and 'at least as advantageous' shall be construed accordingly.

(3) Subject to paragraph (6), where rule 36.14(1)(b) applies, the court will, unless it considers it unjust to do so, order that the claimant is entitled to –

(a) interest on the whole or part of any sum of money (excluding interest) awarded at a rate not exceeding 10% above base rate(GL) for some or all of the period starting with the date on which the relevant period expired;

(b) his costs on the indemnity basis from the date on which the relevant period expired;

(c) interest on those costs at a rate not exceeding 10% above base rate(GL); and

(d) an additional amount, which shall not exceed £75,000, calculated by applying the prescribed percentage set out below to an amount which is –

> *(ii) where the claim is only a non-monetary claim, the sum awarded to the claimant by the court in respect of costs –*

It is therefore argued that early Part 36 offers on these cases are essential, as this is now the only way defendants will be encouraged to settle claims, as the costs consequences for the defendant are severe, if the claimant beats its own Part 36 offer at trial. It may be advisable therefore that a realistic Part 36 offer should be made as soon as possible, and as soon as possible after directions have been given and the claim has been allocated to track. As a matter of tactics, the claimant however may wish to wait until the claim has been allocated before making the offer, since if the case is allocated to the multi track, fixed recoverable costs will not apply.

It is important that the Part 36 offer is a realistic one, rather than as a starting point of negotiations. The earlier the Part 36 offer is made, the greater the consequences for the defendant if the offer is not beaten at Trial, and thus the more weight the defendant is likely to give to that offer when considering whether to accept it or not.

Defendant Part 36 Rules In Post July 2013 FRC Cases

It is still the case that for cases that stay allocated to the fast track and thus within fixed recoverable costs, defendant Part 36 offers will still apply and thus still 'bite'. It therefore may still be prudent for the claimant to obtain ATE cover to insure the risk.

Costs consequences following judgment

36.14

(1) Subject to rule 36.14A, this rule applies whereupon judgment being entered:-

(a) a claimant fails to obtain a judgment more advantageous than a defendant's Part 36 offer; or

(1A) For the purposes of paragraph (1), in relation to any money claim or money element of a claim, 'more advantageous' means better in money terms by any amount, however small, and 'at least as advantageous' shall be construed accordingly.

(2) Subject to paragraph (6), where rule 36.14(1)(a) applies, the court will, unless it considers it unjust to do so, order that the defendant is entitled to:-

(a) his costs from the date on which the relevant period expired; and

(b) interest on those costs.

<u>*But if the Defendants' costs*</u>

<u>*45.29F*</u>

(1) In this rule:-

(a) paragraphs (8) and (9) apply to assessments of defendants' costs under Part 36;

2) If, in any case to which this Section applies, the court makes an order for costs in favour of the defendant:-

(a) the court will have regard to; and

(b) the amount of costs ordered to be paid shall not exceed, the amount which would have been payable by the defendant if an order for costs had been made in favour of the claimant at the same stage of the proceedings.

(3) For the purpose of assessing the costs payable to the defendant by reference to the fixed costs in Table 6, Table 6A, Table 6B, Table 6C and Table 6D, "value of the claim for damages" and "damages" shall be treated as references to the value of the claim.

In other words, if the claimant fails to obtain a judgment more advantageous than a defendant's Part 36 offer, then unless the court considers it unjust, the claimant gets the fixed costs under the relevant table up to the stage the case had reached at the end of the relevant period, but must pay the defendant's costs from the end of the relevant period to the date of judgment, subject to capping.

Where a defendant is awarded costs, the maximum amount of costs payable by the claimant to the defendant is the difference between the fixed costs applicable at the date of acceptance less the costs to which the claimant is entitled.

Allocation Post July 2013 cases.

It may be argued therefore, that allocation will become the new battleground between claimants and defendants. Claimants will want the case allocated to the multi track, to escape fixed recoverable costs, and defendants will want the case allocated to the fast track to keep within fixed recoverable costs. The difficulty for claimants is that the Court is now likely to view the majority of slipping and tripping cases as straight forward cases that can be dealt with in the fast track, but CPR 26.8 sets out:-

Matters relevant to allocation to a track

26.8

(1) When deciding the track for a claim, the matters to which the court shall have regard include:-

   (a) the financial value, if any, of the claim;

   (b) the nature of the remedy sought;

   (c) the likely complexity of the facts, law or evidence;

(d) the number of parties or likely parties;

(e) the value of any counterclaim or other Part 20 claim and the complexity of any matters relating to it;

(f) the amount of oral evidence which may be required;

(g) the importance of the claim to persons who are not parties to the proceedings;

(h) the views expressed by the parties; and

(i) the circumstances of the parties.

Given that the court in most cases now allocates initially on paper to a track, it may be a good idea that if, for a claimant, it is a) complex in law, b) complex in fact, c) requires numerous experts, d) is likely to require oral expert evidence, e) is going to last more than one day due to the number of witnesses, the claimant drafts submissions and returns these to the court, with the directions questionnaire and asks for the matter to be listed for a CMC, to determine the issue of track, if the claimant wants the claim to be allocated to the multi track. The general rule is that if the case is likely to last more than one day, it needs to be allocated to the multi track. It may be advisable that if the case is likely to last more than one day, a draft trial timetable is submitted to the court, setting out why and how.

Many more complex slipping and tripping cases, particularly where there may be multiple defendants, more serious injuries or where there are complex disputes of fact should be in the multi track, to allow provision for expert evidence on both fact and causation, if required. Whatever track a case remains in, and even if it remains within FRC, a claimant lawyer still of course has a duty to obtain all appropriate evidence to support the case and investigate to the fullest extent, even if it remains within FRC. It may well be that defendants are prepared to sacrifice their own medical expert to keep cases out of the multi track and in FRC. It will be of interest to see how this develops.

Summary

It seems clear that there are a number of tactical decisions to be made early on in slipping and tripping cases post-Jackson, and in particular issues surrounding allocation of track, when to make a Part 36 offer and when to make applications for disclosure. However, if one makes astute tactical decisions, this will still make this type of work economical for claimant law firms and allow claimants continued access to justice.

UPDATE 2018: Nicole Chapman v Tameside Hospital NHS Foundation Trust (2016)

A defendant which had failed to comply with the Pre-Action Protocol for Personal Injury Claims was ordered to pay the claimant's costs. The defendant had asserted that it had no documents to disclose pre-issue, but subsequently disclosed relevant documents, causing the claimant to discontinue her claim and she was awarded her full costs on an OL claim. This is an important decision of post Jackson cases in a situation whereby early disclosure of documents is withheld and later disclosed in proceedings.

The Judgment said:-

1. *This has been the hearing of an unusual application, certainly not one, which I have come across before. I said somewhat flippantly just before lunch that Deputy District Judge Herzog should have acceded to the parties' application, yesterday, to take this matter before a regional costs judge which would have avoided my having to address this novel but somewhat thorny issue. However I am entirely satisfied it was appropriate for me to deal with it and Judge Herzog's decision was entirely correct.*

2. *It's an occupier's liability claim. The Claimant alleges that she went to the Defendant's A & E Department and whilst there she slipped on a leaflet on the floor (quite probably a solicitor's leaflet advertising their services), as a result of which she fell and*

incurred injuries which are set out in the report, which is on the file, from Dr Ballin.

3. *Occupier's liability claims now, of course, are commenced in the Portal but this case it dropped out of the Portal. Therefore Part 7 proceedings were issued and they proceeded in a fairly normal fashion, but close to trial they were discontinued and that discontinuance followed some discussions between the parties' solicitors. As a result they sent a consent order to the Court on 8th April, which I had to amend because it provided at paragraph 2:*

(It is ordered that) "the Claimant withdraws her claim for damages."

Of course, the Court has got no power to do that, a common error, but being somewhat pedantic I simply converted that into a recording that the Claimant withdrew her claim for damages, but the crucial part of the order was at paragraph 2 of the order as issued:

"The Claimant's entitlement to costs (if any) pursuant to CPR 44.2 and 44.11 and the level of those costs should be dealt with by a hearing, 15th June at 11 a.m."

4. *The provisions of CPR 44.11 are not in fact germane, though they relate to misconduct in relation to assessment proceedings, but the relevant consideration is, of course, CPR 44.2. That starts off headed: "The Court's discretion as to costs, 44.21:*

> *"(1) The Court has discretion as to –*
> *(a) whether costs are payable by one party to another; (b) the amount of those costs; and*
> *(c) when they are to be paid."*

And it goes on at 44.2.4:

"In deciding what order (if any) to make about costs, the

Court will have regard to all the circumstances, including –

(a) the conduct of all the parties;"

And 44.2.5:

> *"The conduct of the parties includes –*
> *(a) conduct before, as well as during, the proceedings and in particular the extent to which the parties followed the Practice Direction – Pre- Action Conduct or any relevant pre-action protocol;*
>
> *(b) whether it was reasonable for a party to raise, pursue or contest a particular allegation or issue;*
> *(c) the manner in which a party has pursued or defended its case or a particular allegation or issue; and*
>
> *(d) whether a Claimant who has succeeded in the claim, in whole or in part, exaggerated its claim."*
>
> *But of course, that final provision is not germane to the issues here.*
>
> *5. And what the Claimant says is that the Defendant's conduct in dealing with this claim has been such that the Court ought to implement the punitive provisions of 44.2.4 and*
>
> *5. The provision of that part of the rules is designed to be part of the Court's cost controlling mechanism and to provide a means whereby the Court can impose a penalty on a party who has mis-conducted litigation. And it does have to be said really here, that the Defendant's conduct of this matter has been entirely unacceptable and egregious. It is typified by the first letter in the bundle.*

6. *The situation here was that this was not an unusual claim. It*

was a claim by somebody who had gone into the Defendant's premises and slipped as a result, she would say, of contamination of the floor. So it is not an unusual or exotic claim, it's the kind of claim which the Courts are fully familiar with and which practitioners dealing with these matters should also be fully familiar with.

7. *The matter is now being dealt with on behalf of the Defendant by Weightmans. At that stage it was being dealt with by the NHS Litigation Authority and I hazard a guess at the number of claims, occupier's liability claims, brought against the Health Service, dealt with by the Litigation Authority must be enormous. They should be familiar with dealing with these claims and appreciate the relevant issues.*

8. *The letter of 16th February, the first correspondence on the matter:*

   "We refer to the above and previous correspondence. We have completed our investigations and confirm liability is denied. Our investigations have revealed that the Trust have no evidence of the incident occurring and therefore, put your client to strict proof that the incident occurred as alleged.

   Please note the Trust have no documents to disclose."
   In an occupier's liability case, of course, the Claimant clearly has to establish that the accident occurred as she alleges. She then has to also satisfy the Court that the occupier of the premises, in this case the Tameside Trust, have not taken such steps as were reasonable to provide for her safety whilst using the premises.

9. *Accordingly the issues which the Court would have to deal with were firstly, whether the accident occurred as claimed as a pure issue of fact and, of course, in relation to that the Defendant may have information in that the accident may have been witnessed by its staff. But often it will be the case that it has no*

direct evidence, in which case its entirely appropriate for it to say to the Claimant "well you prove that it happened". It is in relation to the second element that its response really was entirely unsatisfactory. The Litigation Authority must have been aware that once the Claimant had satisfied the Court that the accident had occurred as she alleged, it was then up to it to establish to the Court's satisfaction that it had a suitable system in place and the Court would clearly expect that system to be documented.

10. *Under the Pre-action Protocol ("PAP") the Trust -- or the Litigation Authority on behalf of the Trust, was under a duty to set out, not on a fully pleaded basis but concisely, what its case was and in particular, was then under an obligation to provide documentation. That is dealt with in the rules under the Pre-action Protocol for PI claims and appears at page 2385 in the present White Book, paragraph 265:*

"The Defendant should also enclose with the response, documents in their possession which are material to the issues between the parties, and which would be likely to be ordered to be disclosed by the Court, either on an application for pre-action disclosure, or on disclosure during proceedings."

Clearly in any proceedings such as this claim the Court would have made an order for standard disclosure. Disclosure would have to be given of any documentation which set out the system and in particular, any records to confirm that the system was indeed being complied with. It is one thing to say we have this system, a piece of paper which says "this is what our system is", it is another thing for the Court to be satisfied that in fact that system is being properly implemented. The obligation was on the Defendants to provide at that early stage that documentation. This reflects the "cards on the table" ethos incorporated into the CPR to try and deal with issues at an early stage and avoid, whenever possible, litigation. It obviously would be somewhat burdensome for the Defendant. It would require somebody at the Trust to go through the documentation to pull out the appropriate pieces of paper. One would not have thought that it would be that difficult, but it was an obligation they were subject to. It is not here a case of the Defendant not dealing with disclosure. The Litigation Authority state in terms "we have no documents to disclose". That, perhaps not unreasonably, was taken by the Claimant's solicitors as an indication, somewhat unbelievably, that in the Defendant did not have any systems, because otherwise they would clearly have documentation to disclose. Had the Defendant failed to address the issue of documentation the Claimant would have probably issued an application for pre action disclosure. Such an application was inappropriate because the Defendant's legal representative had said that the Defendant did not have anydocuments.

11. *So, proceedings were issued, a defence was then filed. The defence again put the Claimant to proof at paragraph 1, but goes on at paragraphs 2(a), 2(c) to set out that it has a proper system in place. Its ays:*

At paragraph 2a "Relevant risk assessments have been performed prior to the Claimant's attendance at the Trust. The Defendant took such care as is reasonable to ensure the Claimant would be reasonably safe when attending the premises" and

At paragraph 2(b) "The Defendant employed contract cleaners to clean the area and regularly inspect it to ensure the floor was clean. In addition all employees are trained to look for and report any hazards."

So the Defendant is specifically pleading that they have a system in place for ensuring, as far as they can, that the premises are safe. It must be borne in mind that the obligation under the1957Actisnotabsolutebutistotakereasonablesteps. That

was fully appreciated by the Claimant's solicitors, who were aware of the Ward v. Tesco decision and cited it repeatedly to the

Defendant's representative.

12. The Court made the usual directions, including a direction for disclosure. The Defendant's first disclosure was made on 5th January 2016 in the usual form. It is important to appreciate that that form was signed -- one never knows who it is signed by because somewhat strangely this form does not mirror the statement of truth provisions which require the name of the signatory to be given, but it is signed on behalf of the Defendant and it states:

"I certify that I fully understand the duty of disclosure and to the best of my knowledge I have carried out that duty. I fully further certify that the list of documents set out in or attached to this form is a complete list of all documents which are or have been in my control and which I am obliged under the order to disclose."

In fact, all of the documents which are listed at page 10 are

 i. *Trust assessments for slips, trips and falls:*

 ii. *Trust's slips, trips and falls policy.*

 iii. *Standard cleaning schedule for Accident & Emergency."*

So they are saying at that stage, not as they had said previously, "we have not got any documents," but they are saying, "we have documents and these are all the relevant documents" and there is a certificate to that effect signed by somebody on behalf of the Defendant.

13. *What then happened is quite clear from the correspondence and documentation which I have been shown, that issues were raised by the Claimant's solicitors and they were then drip-fed further documentation, culminating in the disclosure at the end of February of 2016 of the crucial documentation, which was the Mitie documentation, Mitie being the cleaning contractor engaged by the Defendant to*

whom reference is made in paragraph 2 of the defence. The crucial documents are in fact documents 10 and 11, that is the Mitie cleaning rota for the year from week commencing 15th December 2014 and a copy of Mitie's daily work schedule for the A & E Department. That is the documentation upon which the Defendant is relying to say, not only that it has a proper system in place and has taken reasonable steps to ensure that visitors to its premises are safe, but also that that system is being implemented and is in operation. <u>That documentation should have all been supplied back at the beginning of the proceedings, before issue and clearly demonstrates that the final paragraph of the Litigation Authority's letter of 16th February 2015 is, in pure and simple terms, false.</u>

14. What then happened was that after a further short flurry about photographs, the Claimant's solicitors reviewed the matter, took further instructions and then held discussions which resulted in the discontinuance of the claim, having reached the agreement with Weightmans which was recorded in the order made by me on 8th April.

15. The Defendant's behavious in the conduct of this litigation was entirely unacceptable. It's exactly the type of conduct which Part 44.2 is designed to address. Under the modern costs provisions, of course, the costs sanctions become increasingly important. The Claimant's solicitors are pursuing these matters, PI claims, and at the end of the claim are recovering costs which are fixed and which are not by any stretch of the imagination, generous. There is a danger of -- I am not saying it has happened in this case -- this is a pure inadequacy of approach by the Litigation Authority and the Trust, but there is a danger that defendants and their representatives will cause difficulties in the course of litigation, so as to run up the work which claimant's solicitors are having to do in the knowledge that those solicitors cannot recover costs reflecting that work. And of course, it always

has to be borne in mind the provisions of CPR 1.3, that the parties to litigation have an obligation to assist the Court to further the overriding objective. The overriding objective firstly being to try and avoid costs and the issue of proceedings if at all possible, which is the whole purpose of the pre-action protocol, of course and secondly, when such claims are brought that they be dealt with in an efficient manner, in a proper manner so as to avoid excessive costs, involving public resources, delay and so on.

16. *Various issues have arisen, the first is the question of evidence., Mr Smith makes the valid and very fair point that, strictly, there is no evidence that has been filed by the Claimant in support of his or her contention that the claim would have been abandoned at an early stage had the Defendants produced the documentation which they were under an obligation to produce. Clearly there should have been a statement by Ms Ireland that should have been in proper form and should have been provided. I do not have that. What I do have is a detailed skeleton argument prepared by Ms Ireland, which, whilst it does not bear her signature, does at the end bear her name and is clearly a document produced by her of which she is the author. It is not endorsed with a statement of truth, but of course, I have discretion under Rule 3.10 in relation to errors of procedure and so on and I am satisfied in the circumstance that it is appropriate for me to treat the factual content of that document as evidence. And I am satisfied on the balance of probabilities that had the NHS Litigation Authority produced under the PAP the documentation which they should have produced, i.e. the risk assessments and most crucially the Mitie documentation, then the claim would not have gone any further. There clearly was misconduct on the part of the Defendant.*

17. *The matter does not rest there, however, because this is a fixed costs case and it is suggested by Mr Smith that it is a binary system and that you either get the fixed costs or none at all, the*

fixed costs for a settlement at that stage would have been £3,790. Issues of indemnity also arose, they were in fact raised by me, I set that particular hare running. But I have been referred to, I cannot remember whether it was High Court or Court of Appeal decision, which indicates that the indemnity principle does not apply in cases covered by the fixed costs regime.

MR SMITH: *It is Simon J, sir.*
DISTRICT JUDGE SWINDLEY: *Thank you.*

18. I am satisfied that the provisions of Rule 44.2 can be applied. It would be a nonsensical situation if the rules which are provided by Rule 44.2 to give the Court the power to impose sanctions to penalise those who abuse the system, and clearly there has been abuse here by the Trust and possibly by the Litigation Authority initially representing them. I am certainly not suggesting that Weightmans have been dealing with it improperly, they are obviously having to deal with what information they are supplied. But it would be a nonsensical situation if the rules, in an appropriate case where the fixed costs regime did apply, precluded the Court from imposing the sanctions provided under Rule 44.2 and 44.2, of course, gives the Court an unqualified discretion. I do not accept that I am bound by the Part 45 scales, but I clearly have to bear them in mind. It would be nonsensical if the Claimant's solicitors could achieve a windfall and recover more costs than they would have done had the matter gone to trial or settled in favour of the Claimant at the stage that it was discontinued. That would be absolutely nonsensical.

19. *The approach taken by Ms Ireland in her submission as to costs seems to me entirely appropriate. What she basically says is, had we been successful we would have been awarded our base costs(that is the costs without the added 20% of damages) which at that stage were £3,790, but had we not proceeded*

after we had been supplied with the appropriate documentation by the Trust Litigation Authority, we had already incurred some costs, the scale figure for those would be £950 and the accordingly the appropriate way of dealing with it is to set one against the other and award the Claimant's solicitors £2,840 plus VAT. I am satisfied that is an appropriate way of dealing with the matter and I award that sum, plus the fee for MrBallin'sreport at £426, which I calculate to be a total of £3,834. In relation to the various costs or the Court fees rather, I see that Scott Rees have already written to the Court sending the forms completed by their client to get a return of the fees, she apparently being someone who was exempt from the payment of fees.

20. *Accordingly, I make an order in favour of the Claimant for £3,834.*

UPDATE 2018: Part 36 Offers and Broadhurst v Tan

BROADHURST v TAN (2016), was an important case which set out the principle that, in a fixed costs personal injury claim governed by CPR 45, costs were payable on the indemnity basis, where a party had made a Part 36 offer and then beaten this offer at Trial. The Court said in Broadhurst:-

8. *A new rule 36.14A was also introduced to prescribe the costs consequences following judgment in section IIIA cases. While it modified some aspects of rule 36.14 (which set out the cost consequences following judgment) in fixed costs cases, it left rule 36.14(3) unmodified. Rule 36.14 provided, so far as material:*

"36.14 – Costs consequences following judgment
(1)... (3)
Subject to rule 36.14A, this rule applies where upon judgment being entered...

(b) judgment against the defendant is at least as advantageous to the claimant as the proposals contained in a claimant's part 36 offer.

Subject to paragraph (6), where rule 36.14(1)(b) applies, the court will, unless it considers it unjust to do so, order that the claimant is entitled to –

(a) interest on the whole or part of any sum of money (excluding interest) awarded at a rate not exceeding 10% above base rate for some or all of the period starting with the date on which the relevant period expired;

(b) costs on the indemnity basis from the date on which the relevant period expired;

(c) interest on those costs at a rate not exceeding 10% above base rate and

(d) an additional amount, which shall not exceed £75,000, calculated by applying the prescribed percentage set out below..."

10. Rule 36.14A provided, so far as material:
"36.14A – Costs consequences following judgment where Section IIIA of Part 45 applies

Where a claim no longer continues under the RTA or EL/PL Protocol pursuant to rule 45.29A(1), rule 36.14 applies with the following modifications.

Subject to paragraphs (3), (3A) and (3B) where an order for costs is made pursuant to rule 36.14(2)-

(a) the claimant will be entitled to the fixed costs in Table 6B, 6C or 6D in section IIIA of Part 45 for the stage applicable at the date on which the relevant period expired; and

(b) the claimant will be liable for the defendant's costs from the date on which the relevant period expired to the date of the judgment.

Subject to paragraphs (3A) and (3B) where the claimant fails to obtain a judgment more advantageous than the defendant's Protocol offer -

> *(a) the claimant will be entitled to the applicable Stage 1 and Stage 2 fixed costs in Table 6 or Table 6A in Section III of Part 45; and*
>
> *(b) the claimant will be liable for the defendant's costs from the date on which the Protocol offer is deemed to be made to the date of judgment; and*

Fixed costs shall be calculated by reference to the amount which is awarded.

Where the court makes an order for costs in favour of the defendant —

> (a) *the court will have regard to; and*
> (b) *the amount of costs ordered shall not exceed,*

the fixed costs in Table 6B, 6C or 6D in Section IIIA of Part 45 applicable at the date of judgment, less the fixed costs to which the claimant is entitled under paragraph (2) or (3).

The parties are entitled to disbursements allowed in accordance with rule 45.29I incurred in any period for which costs are payable to them."

"I would allow the appeal in the case of Broadhurst and dismiss the appeal in the case of Smith largely for the reasons stated by Mr Williams.

If rule 45.29B stood alone, then subject to various rules in Part 45 which are immaterial, the only costs allowable in a section IIIA case to a claimant who was awarded costs following judgment in his favour would be "(a) the fixed costs in rule 45.29C and (b) disbursements in accordance with rule 45.29I". But rule 45.29B does not stand alone. The need to take account of Part 36 offers in section IIIA cases was recognised by the draftsman of the rules. Indeed, rule 36.14A is headed "costs consequences following judgment where section IIIA of Part 45 applies". Rule 45.29F (8) provides that, where a Part 36 offer is accepted in a section IIIA case, "rule 36.10A will apply instead of this rule". And rule 45.29F(9) provides that, where in such a case upon judgment being entered the claimant fails to obtain a judgment more advantageous than the claimant's Part 36 offer, "rule 36.14A will apply instead of this rule". Rule 45.29F does not, however, make provision as to what should happen where the claimant makes a successful Part 36 offer.

Mr Laughland submits that, since rule 45.29F makes no such provision, the basic or general rule in rule 45.29B that the only costs allowable are fixed costs and disbursements carries the day. But that is to ignore rule 36.14A which is headed "Costs consequences following judgment where section IIIA of Part 45 applies". Rule 36.14A(1) provides that in a section IIIA case "rule 36.14 applies with the following modifications". As we have seen, rule 36.14(3) provides that, where a claimant makes a successful Part 36 offer, the court will, unless it considers it unjust to do so, order that the claimant is entitled to four enhanced benefits including "(b) his costs on the indemnity basis from the date on which the relevant period expired".

The effect of rules 36.14 and 36.14A when read together is that, where a claimant makes a successful Part 36 offer, he is entitled to costs assessed on the indemnity basis. Thus, rule 36.14 is modified only to the extent stated by 36.14A. Since rule 36.14(3) has not been modified by rule 36.14A, it continues to have full force and effect. The tension between rule 45.29B and rule 36.14A must, therefore, be resolved in favour of rule 36.14A. I reach this conclusion as a straightforward matter of interpretation and without recourse to the canon of construction that, where there is a conflict between a specific provision and a general provision, the former takes precedence. As we have seen, there is disagreement as to which is the relevant general provision in the present context. Mr Williams submits that it is rule 36.14; and Mr Laughland submits that it is rule 45.29B. I do not find it necessary to resolve this difference.

Rule 36.14A(8) provides further support for my conclusion. This provision states that in a section IIIA case the parties (i.e. claimant as well as defendant) are entitled to disbursements allowed in accordance with rule 45.29I in any period for which costs are payable to them. This reflects rule 45.29B(b). If, as Mr Laughland contends, rule 45.29B prevailed over rule 36.14A in any event, this provision would have been unnecessary. It is significant that rule 36.14A does not contain a provision which reflects rule 45.29B(a) and 45.29C. In my view, the fact that rule 36.14A contains provision for payment of disbursements in accordance with rule 45.29B(b), but not for payment of fixed costs in accordance with rule 45.29B(a) confirms that the interpretation that I have adopted above is correct.

I find yet further support for the conclusion that I have reached in the wider contextual points made by Mr Williams to which I have referred at para 13 above which it is unnecessary to repeat.

For all these reasons, I do not consider that there is any doubt as to the true meaning of these rules. The tension is clearly resolved in favour of rule 36.14A. If that were wrong, then it would be legitimate to use the Explanatory Memorandum as an aid to construction (this was not the Explanatory Note to the statutory instrument). That is because the three conditions specified by Lord Browne-Wilkinson in Pepper v Hart [1993] AC 593 would be satisfied. First, the rules would, in material part, be obscure and/or ambiguous. Secondly, the Explanatory Memorandum was prepared by the Ministry of Justice (the promoter of the rules) and was laid before Parliament together with the 2013 Amendment Rules. I can see no difference in principle between a statement made in Parliament by a Minister or other promotor of a Bill and an explanatory memorandum laid before Parliament by the promotor of rules. The Rules are subject to the negative resolution procedure. Parliament has no power to amend the Rules, but could have annulled them if it had wished to do so. Thirdly, the statement in the Explanatory Memorandum relied on by the claimants is clear on the issue which arises on this appeal".

The Jackson report does propose change to the *Broadhurst* rules and says:-

Broadhurst v Tan and the effect of an order for indemnity costs. The one issue, which cannot be ducked, however, is Broadhurst v Tan [2016] EWCA Civ 94; [2016] 1 WLR 1928. This decision, unless its effect is modified by rule change, will impact upon fixed costs generally. This issue is equally important in relation to higher value claims, but I deal with it here and will not repeat the discussion in later chapters. Views on this issue are sharply divided:

*(i) **Nine of my assessors consider that, although CPR Part 36 must continue to bring rewards for claimants who make effective Part 36 offers, in the context of a fixed costs regime it would be better for there to be a percentage uplift on the fixed costs rather than an order for indemnity costs.** This will avoid the need for a detailed assessment of costs. Also, it will provide certainty for litigants. Certainty is an essential feature of an FRC regime. As to the level of percentage uplift, views range between 25% and 50%.*

(ii) Five of my assessors take the opposite view. Nicholas Bacon QC writes:

"I do not agree with the proposal that we do away with the Broadhurst indemnity costs order. These cases on indemnity costs are not clogging up the courts with detailed assessments. It is a powerful message for a party to consider rejection/acceptance. A 30% enhancement is not sufficient to redress the failure to accept an offer. It ignores the fact that as between solicitor and client more than the fixed costs will have been incurred by the client. Why should a client not be entitled to be reimbursed for their actual legal spend, rather than fixed costs, where a party has misconducted

themselves or caused a party to incur costs unnecessarily because an earlier offer should have been accepted."

*I have set out the competing arguments, because this is the only issue on which my assessors are sharply divided. After considering the powerful arguments on both sides, on balance, for the reasons set out in sub-paragraph (i) above, **I favour replacing indemnity costs with a percentage uplift of 30% or perhaps 40%. BUT this is a clear issue of policy, which will need to be addressed in the consultation exercise following this report".***

PAD application costs

Sharp v Leeds City Council held that the fixed costs regime applicable to the Pre-action Protocol for Low Value Personal Injury (Employers' Liability and Public Liability) Claims applied to the costs of an application for pre-action disclosure by a claimant even where the claim had started off under the protocol but was no longer continuing under it when the application was made. However the Court said that the fixed costs regime could be dis-applied where there was unreasonable behavior:-

38. *But in my judgment the answer to this submission lies not in subjecting the fixed costs regime to an implied exception for PAD applications which exposed recalcitrant defendants to an altogether higher but variable level of recoverable costs liability, to be determined by assessment. Rather, the answer lies in the availability of an application under Part 45.29J, if exceptional circumstances can be shown or, for the future, in a recognition by the Rule Committee that the fixed costs regime needs to be kept under review, and defects in it remedied by adjustment of the fixed allowances where that can be shown to be justified.*

39. ***It may well be that the frequency with which defendants fail to comply with their Protocol disclosure obligations may make it difficult to pass the exceptional circumstances hurdle in Part***

45.29J, although I would not regard deliberate disregard of those obligations as unexceptional merely because it was frequently encountered. It may be that the very limited recovery of expenditure on a PAD application under the fixed costs regime means that such applications are not as effective as a means of sanctioning breach of Protocol disclosure obligations as they should be. If that is made good by appropriate evidence, then it seems to me that some consideration by way of review to the establishment of a more generous, but still fixed, recovery of costs of such applications would be justified.

40. *By contrast, to throw open PAD applications generally to the recovery of assessed costs would in my view be to risk giving rise to an undesirable form of satellite litigation in which there would be likely to be incentives for the incurring of disproportionate expense, which is precisely what the fixed costs regime, viewed as a whole, is designed to avoid. **The fixed costs regime inevitably contains swings and roundabouts, and lawyers who assist claimants by participating in it are accustomed to taking the rough with the smooth, in pursuing legal business which is profitable overall.***

Bird v Acorn (2017) - a disposal hearing was a "trial" where a personal injury claim had started under the Pre-Action Protocol for Low Value Personal Injury (Employers Liability and Public Liability) Claims and had settled after judgment but before trial. Consequently, the correct scale of fixed costs was contained in the third column of part B of Table 6D. The Court said:-

22. *Finally, there are passages in Jackson LJ's Interim Report, in particular at paragraph 1.12 and following in chapter 22, which suggest that the three columns in what is now Table 6D part B were intended usually to be steps in a ladder. But those general observations do not detract from the interpretation of the definition of trial at which I have arrived. In every case where a claimant obtains judgment for damages to be assessed, followed by a disposal hearing for that assessment, there will be a progression from column 1 (which comes into force when proceedings are issued) to column*

3, when the disposal hearing is listed. The fact that column 2 is jumped over because there is no intermediate allocation to the fast track seems to me to be just one of those events which means that the three columns will not always be triggered in succession. But that by no means undermines the good sense of a conclusion that, once there has been a listing for a disposal hearing, column 3 is triggered.

CHAPTER THREE
PUBLIC LIABILITY AND HIGHWAYS
CLAIMS POST-JACKSON: THE PORTALS

The public liability (PL) portals came into effect on 31 July 2013. Any book looking at slipping and tripping claims post-Jackson, would not be complete without an examination of the portals, and perhaps more importantly for claimant practitioners, the exit points from the Low Value Portals. What stays in, and what comes out of the portal, may be a key decision for some claimant law firms as to whether they feel it is economical to undertake this type of work.

It is arguable that the success of the RTA portal, has encouraged the MOJ to introduce the Low Value Portal for slipping and tripping claims. However, early indications seems to be that the dropout rates from the portal are quite substantial, which is probably for two reasons; a) the timescales for the defendant to investigate cases in the portal are inadequate, and b) slipping and tripping cases are evidentially more complex than road traffic cases, hence it is much more difficult to determine the issue of liability.

If a slip or tripping claim starts in the Low Value Portal and liability is admitted, then the case will remain in the Portal to the conclusion, subject to other dropout points. If liability is denied, then the case will exit the Portal, and ordinarily, proceed in Fixed Recoverable costs, dis-cussed in other Chapters.

The relevant provisions of the Portal for highways and public liability claims are as follows:

Which Claims Do The Portals Apply To?

Pre-Action Protocol for Low Value Personal Injury (Public Liability) Claims

A new Pre-Action Protocol is introduced which will apply to most public liability claims up to the value of £25,000 in respect of an accident occurring on or after 31 July 2013 or, in a disease claim, where no letter of claim has been sent to the defendant before 31 July 2013.

What Is A PL Claim Within The Meaning Of The Portal?

(1) 'public liability claim'—

> *(a) means a claim for damages for personal injuries arising out of a breach of a statutory or common law duty of care made against:-*

> > *(i) a person other than the claimant's employer; or*

> > *(ii) the claimant's employer in respect of matters arising other than in the course the claimant's employment;*

> **but does not include a claim for damages arising from a disease that the claimant is alleged to have contracted as a consequence of breach of statutory or common law duties of care,** *other than a physical or psychological injury caused by an accident or other single event.*

Admissions/Causation

1.1 In this Protocol—

> *(1) 'admission of liability' means the defendant admits that—*

> > *(a) the breach of duty occurred;*

(b) the defendant thereby caused some loss to the claimant, the nature and extent of which is not admitted; and

(c) the defendant has no accrued defence to the claim under the Limitation Act 1980;

It is arguable that if causation is denied, then the claim should exit the portal i.e. any allegation that the claimant was injured elsewhere or that there was other causation of injury. Many insurers will not admit liability until they have seen medical records to check causation, hence it is arguable that most claims will exit the portal.

One may find some insurers test portal admissions for commercial reasons, even when there is doubt over causation, but one will find that the majority of claims will exit for this reason.

The Exemptions from the Portal

4.3 This Protocol does not apply to a claim—

(1) where the claimant or defendant acts as personal representative of a deceased person;

(2) where the claimant or defendant is a protected party as defined in rule 21.1(2);

(3) in the case of a public liability claim, where the defendant is an individual ('individual' does not include a defendant who is sued in their business capacity or in their capacity as an office holder);

(4) where the claimant is bankrupt;

(5) where the defendant is insolvent and there is no identifiable insurer;

(6) in the case of a disease claim, where there is more than one defendant;

(7) for personal injury arising from an accident or alleged breach of duty occurring outside England and Wales;

(8) for damages in relation to harm, abuse or neglect of or by children or vulnerable adults;

(9) which includes a claim for clinical negligence

Thus any claims for slipping and tripping against individuals will not commence in the Low Value Portal, and a letter of claim in accordance with the pre-action Protocol will be sent in the normal way.

Completion of the Claim notification form

6.1(1) The claimant must complete and send—

(a) the CNF to the defendant's insurer, if known; and

(b) the Defendant Only Claim notification form ("defendant Only CNF") to the defendant,

but the requirement to send the form to the defendant may be ignored in a disease claim where the CNF has been sent to the insurer and the defendant has been dissolved, is insolvent or has ceased to trade.

(2) If—

(a) the insurer's identity is not known; or

(b) the defendant is known not to hold insurance cover, the CNF must be sent to the defendant.

Where the insurer's identity is not known, the claimant must make a reasonable attempt to identify the insurer.

Thus, for an occupiers liability claim under the 1957 Act, a reasonable search for the defendant's insurer must be undertaken. This may involve writing to the defendant and asking them to identify the relevant insurer.

Failure to complete the Claim notification form

6.7
Where the defendant considers that inadequate mandatory information has been provided in the CNF, that shall be a valid reason for the defendant to decide that the claim should no longer continue under this Protocol.

Thus, it is essential that the claimant puts a detailed description of the accident circumstances in the CNF, together with detailed allegations of negligence. One must remember that this is a document verified by a statement of truth and the claimant may be cross-examined on the basis of this document at trial. It is therefore essential that care be taken to draft the CNF. The claimant should check, read and approve the CNF, and especially the accident circumstances and injuries, before it is disclosed to the defendant. There are costs consequences if the Court finds the claim exited the portal due to inadequate information on the CNF:-

6.8 Rule 45.24(2) sets out the sanctions available to the court where it considers that the claimant provided inadequate information in the CNF.

Portal Exit Points

6.13
The claim will no longer continue under this protocol where the defendant, within the relevant period in paragraph 6.11:-

(1) makes an admission of liability but alleges contributory negligence;

(2) does not complete and send the CNF response;

(3) does not admit liability; or

(4) notifies the claimant that the defendant considers that—

> *(a) there is inadequate mandatory information in the CNF; or*

> *(b) if proceedings were issued, the small claims track would be the normal track for that claim*

One must bear in mind, that for many of the exit points, it will be up to the claimant to exit the claim from the Portal, by notifying the defendant, if it is does not time-out automatically on the Portal. If the claim exits the Portal, it will continue under the *Personal Injury Pre-Action Protocol.*

Thus any argument of contributory negligence will automatically exit the claim from the portal.

Investigation Times

6.11 The defendant must complete the 'Response' section of the CNF ("the CNF response") and send it to the claimant:-

(b) in the case of a public liability claim, within 40 days of the step taken pursuant to paragraph 6.1

It is therefore notable that the defendant's timescale to investigate the claim is very limited indeed. This is the reason, and it appears that the majority of claims exit the portal in any event, given the short timescales to investigate the claim.

Other Exit Points for Costs Payments

For non-payment of Stage 1 fixed costs

6.16   *Except where the claimant is a child,* **where liability is admitted the defendant must pay the Stage 1 fixed costs in rule 45.XX within 10 days after receiving the Stage 2 Settlement Pack.**

6.17   <u>*Where the defendant fails to pay the Stage 1 fixed costs within the period specified in paragraph 6.15 the claimant may give written notice that the claim will no longer continue under this Protocol.*</u> *Unless the claimant's notice is sent to the defendant within 10 days after the expiry of the period in paragraph 6.15 the claim will continue under this Protocol.*

Non-settlement payment by the defendant at the end of Stage 2

7.53   *Except where the claimant is a child the defendant must pay to the claimant—*

   (1)   *the final offer of damages made by the defendant in the Court Proceedings Pack (Part A and Part B) Form less any —*

      (a)   *deductible amount which is payable to the CRU;*

      and

      (b)   *previous interim payment(s);*

   (2)   *any unpaid Stage 1 fixed costs in rule 45.XX;*

   (3)   *the Stage 2 fixed costs in rule 45.XX; and*

   (4)   *the disbursements in rule 45.XX that have been agreed.*

> **7.58** *Where the defendant does not comply with paragraphs 7.54 or 7.56 the claimant may give written notice that the claim will no longer continue under this Protocol and start proceedings under Part 7 of the CPR*

It should be noted that the onus is again on the claimant to exit the claim from the portal. It is therefore important that when dealing with claims post-Jackson, firms have a robust system in place, for spotting the exit points and ensuring they are not missed. Missing any exit point is likely to be very costly for the claimant's solicitor.

Exit Points – Interim Payments

Interim payment of £1,000

> *7.17*
> *(1) Where paragraph 7.12 applies the defendant must pay £1,000 within 10 days of receiving the Interim Settlement Pack.*
>
> *(2) Sub-paragraph (1) does not apply in a claim in respect of a disease to which the Pneumoconiosis etc. (Workers' Compensation) Act 1979 applies unless there is a valid CRU certificate showing no deduction for recoverable lump sum payments.*

Interim payment of more than £1,000

> *7.18 Subject to paragraphs 7.19 and 7.21, where the claimant has requested an interim payment of more than £1,000 the defendant must pay—*
>
> *(1) the full amount requested less any deductible amount which is payable to the CRU;*
>
> *(2) the amount of £1,000; or*
>
> *(3) some other amount of more than £1,000 but less than the*

amount requested by the claimant,
within 15 days of receiving the Interim Settlement Pack.

7.26 Where the defendant does not comply with paragraphs 7.17 or 7.18 the claimant may start proceedings under Part 7 of the CPR and apply to the court for an interim payment in those proceedings.

7.27 Where the defendant does comply with paragraph 7.18(2) or (3) but the claimant is not content with the amount paid, the claimant may still start proceedings. However, the court will order the defendant to pay no more than the Stage 2 fixed costs where the court awards an interim payment of no more than the amount offered by the defendant or the court makes no award.

7.28 Where paragraph 7.26 or 7.27 applies the claimant must give notice to the defendant that the claim will no longer continue under this Protocol. Unless the claimant's notice is sent to the defendant within 10 days after the expiry of the period in paragraphs 7.17, 7.18 or 7.23 as appropriate, the claim will continue under this Protocol.

Exits from the Portal – A Warning

The Court is not likely to look favourably on claims that have exited the portal purely for costs purposes and there are a number of warnings enshrined in the Low Value Portal in this regard and these may be summarised as follows:-

7.59   Where the claimant gives notice to the defendant that the claim is unsuitable for this Protocol (for example, because there are complex issues of fact or law or where claimants contemplate applying for a Group Litigation Order) then the claim will no longer continue under this Protocol. However, where the court considers that the claimant acted unreasonably in giving such notice it will award no more than the fixed costs in rule 45.

What happens if the claim stays with the Portal?

OL/PL claims that stay within the portal are likely to be outside the scope of this book, given that they will be for liability admitted cases, with no causation issues, which then proceed to negotiation as to quantum arguments only. This book is concerned with liability and causation arguments, which do not fall within the scope of the Low Value Portal. However, for the sake of reference a copy of the Low Value Portal Protocol for liability admitted claims could be found at:

http://www.justice.gov.uk/courts/procedure-rules/civil/protocol/pre-action-protocol-for-low-value-personal-injury-employers-liability-and-public-liability-claims#6.13

Conclusions

It may be argued that the Low Value Portal introduced in 2010 for RTA claims and then July 2013 for PL claims is not suitable system for dealing with slipping and tripping claims. These claims tend to be far more complex on liability and causation, with more complex injuries. The timescales for the defendant to investigate cases are inadequate with the portal and the fees proposed in the system for claimant lawyers to investigate complex quantum disputes are inadequate. These changes, which have been in place for almost a year, invariably, result in some claimant law firms employing more junior fee earners with less experience to run such cases and less involvement of Counsel. In the end, this can be counterproductive since the weaker cases are not 'weeded out' as quickly as they may have with the involvement of Counsel or more experienced fee earners within the claimant law firm. This ultimately increases costs for the insurers who have to investigate more claims, which may have been dropped more quickly with more experienced fee earners, under the old system.

CHAPTER FOUR
PUBLIC LIABILITY AND HIGHWAYS
CLAIMS POST-JACKSON:
CAUSATION AND INITIAL LIABILITY
INVESTIGATIONS

Causation is one of the most important aspects when considering any highways slipping or tripping claim. The reason of course for this is that even if the claimant can succeed on the issue of breach of duty, the claimant still has to prove causation in relation to the injuries sustained. This becomes even more important when the credibility of the claimant is at issue between the parties.

The claimant of course will have to prove legal and medical causation on the balance of probability. Establishing causation at an early stage in the case will be as important as establishing breach of duty, given that if the claimant's case fails on the issues of causation, there is little point in establishing breach of duty in the first instance.

This chapter will therefore concentrate solely on investigating causation in relation to highways slipping and tripping claims and occupiers claims and focus on the early investigations to be undertaken in relation to such cases at the outset.

Early Investigation

Early investigation of causation is always going to be key in relation to a highways slipping and tripping case. This will be particularly important if the defendant puts you on notice that causation is going to be an issue.

This inevitably leads to the question as to how causation can be invest-igated in relation to such a case at an early stage and how can it be investigated economically, particularly with reference to fixed costs and portal costs that have been discussed in chapters one, two and three of this book.

The issue of causation can be investigated economically in the following ways:-

Medical Causation

The claimant's solicitor will wish to obtain the claimant's general practitioner records and hospital records at the first opportunity, particularly if it is suggested that the claimant had tripped or fallen elsewhere i.e. not in the hole that the claimant alleges. The claimant's solicitor should carefully go through the claimant's contemporaneous GP and hospital records, as they will often provide clues as to the mechanism of the fall. In particular if the claimant's solicitor is looking for confirmation that the claimant tripped over and the mechanism of the accident described by the claimant is the one recorded in the contemporaneous GP or hospital notes.

If there is any variation in the notes careful instructions will need to be taken from the claimant to the reason for any inconsistencies and some of the following are examples from practice:-

- The claimant says that they have tripped over a hole in the street and the local authority is sued for breach of duty under the Highways Act 1980 but the contemporaneous medical records suggest that the claimant fell at home carrying a child.

- The claimant suggests that they tripped up in a nightclub on liquid and injured their ankle, yet the contemporaneous hospital records suggest that the claimant fell in the street on the way home.

One has to bear in mind that sometimes the treating medical practitioner in a rush at the Accident & Emergency Department or the hospital doctor may get it wrong in the heat of the moment but the claimant's lawyer should be particularly cautious if the mechanism of the accident described has been described incorrectly to both the GP and the treating doctor in the Accident & Emergency Department. If there are any inconsistencies in contemporaneous medical records the claimant's solicitor can sometimes seek to interview the treating GP or hospital doctor in order to confirm if there is any explanation for the notes being incorrect.

Consider the mechanism of the claimant's fall if there are inconsistencies between the GP and the hospital notes. For example, if the claimant states that they tripped over on their right foot in the accident report form but the medical records suggest that the claimant had tripped up on their left foot and these are recorded contemporaneously post-accident this should give rise to caution. It is of course the case that sometimes there are credible explanations for inconsistencies but in the writer's experience the courts tend to treat contemporaneous medical records as having a degree of credibility given that they are recorded shortly after the accident and often before it is known that a claim is being made arising out of a slip, trip or fall.

It may be argued that it is often very difficult for a claimant lawyer to get over serious inconsistencies as to the recording of the mechanism of the accident, without any supporting evidence in respect of the same. If someone has slipped or tripped in the street over an alleged defect caused by the local authority and broken their ankle, and there are clear photographs of the defect, this of course does not automatically mean that the claimant has slipped as suggested and it is always possible that the injury could have been caused elsewhere.

Some commentators have argued that fraud in this area is on the increase given the tightening of the insurer's investigations into whiplash type fraud, and claimant lawyers need to be very careful it may be argued to ensure that the claimant's evidence is credible in relation to the mechanism of the slip, trip or fall.

Recording The Accident Circumstances – The Contemporaneous Version of Events

It is extremely important that the claimant's solicitor obtain from the outset an extremely detailed version of events from the claimant to the mechanism of the accident, and exactly how the injury was sustained, that can be tested later to test the credibility of the first version of events given by the claimant.

Arguably this is even more important now since the first version given by the claimant recorded in the claim notification form has to be verified by a Statement of truth.

It is important that the claim notification form version of events gives enough information to the defendant to investigate the claim at the outset, and some of the following information and questions may be useful when taking instructions from the claimant on a slip, trip or fall case at the outset.

For A Highways Act Claim

For a claim under the Highways Act 1980 the following questions are likely to be asked of the claimant at the outset of the case:-

- Where exactly did the accident happen?

- Did it happen on the highway?

- Does the defendant dispute that the accident happened on the highway?

- What type of footwear was the claimant wearing, was the claimant carrying any items or were there any other factors which could have contributed to the accident by the claimant?

- Had the claimant consumed alcohol and if so, how much and

when?

- How did the accident occur in the claimant's own words?

- Did the accident happen in the road or on the pavement or on some public land?

- What exactly caused the claimant to trip, slip or fall?

- Had the claimant seen the defect before and if so when? Was it reported and if so, to whom?

- Was the defect repaired post-accident and if so, when?

- Was the accident reported and if so, when and to whom?

- If the defect was reported what action was taken, when and by whom?

- Is the defect still there and if so when did the claimant last see it?

- What was the size of the defect that caused the claimant to slip, trip or fall in terms of height, width and length?

- Was the claimant running or walking at the time of the accident?

- Were there any witnesses to the accident?

- Are there any witnesses who can say if the defect was present pre-accident and if so, for how long was the defect present pre-accident?

- Is the claimant aware of any other similar incident?

This is a starting point to investigations when considering a claim under the Highways Act 1980.

Occupiers' Liability Act 1957 Claim

At the outset of the case, some of the following questions may be relevant in relation to Occupiers' Liability Act 1957 questions:-

- Where exactly did the accident happen?

- What type of footwear was the claimant wearing, was the claimant carrying any items or were there any other factors which could have contributed to the accident by the claimant?

- Had the claimant consumed alcohol and if so, how much and when?

- How did the accident occur in the claimant's own words?

- Who was the owner of the land where the accident took place?

- What caused the claimant to trip, fall or slip?

- Had the claimant seen the defect before and if so, when, was it reported and by whom?

- Was the defect repaired post-accident and if so, when?

- Was the accident reported and if so, when and to whom?

- If the defect was reported what action was taken, when and by whom?

- If the defect still there and if so, when did the claimant last see it?

- What was the size of the defect that cause the slip, trip or fall in terms of height, width and length?

- Was the claimant running or walking at the time of the accident?

- Were there any witnesses to the accident?

- Are there any witnesses who can say if the defect was present pre-accident and if so, for how long had the defect been present pre-accident?

- Is the claimant aware of any other similar incidents?

Defective Premises Act 1972 Claims Initial Investigations

Finally if the claimant is bringing a claim under the Defective Premises Act 1972 some of the following questions may be useful at the outset when investigating the issue of liability:-

- Where exactly did the accident happen?

- What was the date of the accident?

- Did the defect arise during the term of a Lease?

- Did the landlord have a duty to repair under the Lease?

- Did the landlord have a right of entry to repair or maintain?

- Did the landlord have actual or constructive notice of the defect prior to the accident?

- What type of footwear was the claimant wearing? Was the claimant carrying any items or were there any other factors that could have contributed to the accident by the claimant?

- Had the claimant consumed alcohol and if so, how much and when?

- What caused the claimant to slip, trip or fall?

- Had the claimant seen the defect before and if so, when was it reported and to whom?

- Was the defect repaired post-accident and if so, when?

- Was the accident reported and if so, when and to whom?

- If a defect was reported what action was taken, when and by whom?

- Is the defect still there and if so, when did the claimant last see it?

- What was the size of the defect that caused the claimant to slip, trip or fall in terms of height, width and length?

- Was the claimant running or walking at the time of the accident?

- Were there any witnesses to the accident?

- Are there any witnesses who can say if the defect was present pre-accident and if so for how long was the defect present pre-accident?

- Is the claimant aware of any other similar incidents?

Causation – The Common Themes

Whether one is investigating a defective premises claim, an occupiers' claim or a highways claim, common themes often arise in terms of the issue of causation and whether the breach of duty contributed to the injuries sustained. Some of these may be broadly defined as follows:-

- Was the claimant running or walking at the time of the accident? It is common sense that lots of accidents are caused through people running rather than walking. At the outset of the claim detailed questions should be taken from the claimant as to whether they were running or walking when the accident took place. If the claimant was running when the accident took place careful consideration should be given to possible findings of contributory negligence.

- Had the claimant consumed alcohol and if so, how much and when? This question will be particularly relevant if the claimant had consumed a lot of alcohol or the accident has occurred in licensed premises or if the claimant had been drinking prior to the accident for a specific period. It may be argued that claimant lawyers should be particularly wary of claimants who have consumed a large amount of alcohol prior to a fall, as this may sound in contributory negligence, if not to extinguish any finding of liability on behalf of the defendant entirely, if the claimant was severely intoxicated at the time of the accident.

- In order to investigate the issues, careful instructions should be taken from the claimant as to how much alcohol had been consumed prior to the accident and in particular one should look at the hospital and GP notes for any contemporaneous records as to whether the claimant had been drinking or not prior to the accident.

- Statements should also be taken from witnesses, family and friends in relation to how much alcohol had been consumed prior to a fall.

- Drinking a substantial amount of alcohol it may be argued will not always be fatal to a claim, given alcohol affects different people in different ways, but if there is any dispute that the claimant was drunk, then medical evidence should be sought as to how the level of alcohol consumed prior to the accident would have contributed to the fall, if at all.

- Lawyers should be particularly aware of a claimant who says they were not drunk in the initial accident questionnaire and the medical records later reveal that in fact the claimant had been drinking.

- Did the claimant trip? In terms of the credibility of tripping claims, one needs to ask the claimant carefully at the outset of the claim how the tripping incident occurred for example did the claimant trip with the left or the right foot, did the foot go entirely into the hole and what caused the claimant to trip, did the claimant's foot get caught on the edge of the defect, and in which direction did the claimant fall?

- Does the claimant's version of events make sense in terms of the mechanism of the tripping claim? For example, if the claimant's foot gets caught on the edge of a defect in the highway, they are likely to fall forwards and not sideways. Whereas if the claimant puts their foot in an open manhole cover they are likely to fall to the side given their entire body weight will have been taken away from them and they will fall towards the side by which the foot has fallen into the manhole. When looking at the claimant's version of events ask yourself does it make sense?

- Was this a slipping incident? If the claimant has slipped, if someone slips, it may be argued that one generally would expect the witnesses evidence to be that their foot had gone from underneath them, and a witness will usually describe a lack of grip under foot or similar prior to the fall and they may describe "their feet going from underneath them".

- It is always important to establish which foot the claimant slipped on. Was it the claimant's left foot or their right foot and again is their version of events credible with regards to the way that they fell and the way that they landed following the fall?

- Was the claimant wearing appropriate footwear? It is always important to establish this at the outset of the claim. For example if the accident occurred in a sports hall and the claimant was participating in sport, was the claimant wearing appropriate training shoes with an appropriate grip? It may be argued, that there is of course nothing wrong with a claimant wearing high heeled shoes on a night out socialising with friends, but in certain circumstances and in particular when undertaking sports or the like, it may be appropriate and may sound in contributory negligence if the claimant was wearing inappropriate footwear for the task.

Handrails?

If the claimant has fallen down a set of stairs, it will be particularly important to check that the claimant was holding the handrail when the accident happened. If there were handrails down both sides of the stairs and the claimant was not utilising the handrail again it may be argued that this could sound in contributory negligence. If the claimant has not used the handrail it will be important to establish why. For example, if the claimant was carrying heavy bags down a set of stairs or an escalator at a train station and there were lifts that the claimant could have used instead, why did the claimant choose to use the stairway rather than the lift and risk falling?

If the claimant was in licensed premises and has slipped on a stairway, not holding the handrail and was attempting to carry drinks on a tray down the stairway, is there another route that the claimant could have taken to have avoided using the stairway?

If handrails are available, it is therefore essential to check that the claimant was utilising the handrail appropriately.

Was the Claimant Carrying Any Items?

It will also be important, to check that the claimant was not carrying any inappropriate items down a stairway at the time the accident happened. For example, was the claimant carrying a child or attempting to carry heavy items down a stairway which could have contributed to the fall?

It is important that when considering liability in a highway slipping or tripping case, the claimant's lawyer takes a step back from the evidence and looks to see what other factors could have caused or contributed to the accident, and if so do these sound in breach of duty against the defendant?

Was the Claimant Aware of the Defect?

It is important to ask the claimant at the outset of the case, if they were previously aware of the defect or had seen it in the past. If there is a particularly large defect, for example, in the highway and the claimant has seen the defect or walked past it every day and then suddenly tripped over it, this of course may give rise to an argument from the defendant that the defect was there, the claimant was aware of it and it was there to be seen.

This is of course very different to the argument where the claimant has not seen the defect before and it has suddenly appeared in the highway and again it may be argued that if the claimant is aware of a defect prior to the accident and they have fallen over it despite seeing it, this may sound in contributory negligence.

Summary

Therefore, when assessing claims at the outset, it is important that the claimant's lawyer looks at all the potential contributory factors to an accident when looking at the issue of causation.

Given that the claim notification form is now verified with a statement of truth, it is essential that detailed instructions are taken from the claimant at the outset of the claim as to the mechanism of the accident and the way in which it was caused and if there are any inconsistencies or any concerns the claimant's general practitioner and hospital records are obtained at the first opportunity in order to check the consistency of events.

Post-Jackson and in fixed costs unless there are credible explanations for inconsistencies, the claimant's lawyer may well be wary of progressing claims that fall outside the portal in fixed costs where there are such serious inconsistencies.

The claimant's solicitor must also ensure that the version provided to the GP or Orthopaedic Surgeon is detailed and the claimant's lawyer should check the consistency of the version given to the claimant's medical expert as compared to the version that was given to the claimant's lawyer at the outset of the case and any inconsistencies in this are addressed urgently at the outset of the case.

It may be argued that there is little room within a fixed costs regime to run cases where there are serious inconsistencies as to legal or medical causation between the version of events in the claim notification form, the GP records, the A&E notes, and the version that is given to the claimant's medical expert.

If there are serious inconsistencies in the version of events provided and without explanation, the claimant's lawyer may at this stage, give some serious consideration as to whether it is a claim that should be litigated.

CHAPTER FIVE
DEALING WITH OCCUPIERS' LIABILITY CLAIMS: THE LAW, CASE SUMMARIES AND GATHERING EVIDENCE – UPDATED 2018 TO INCLUDE MCGEOWN DEFENCES, AND UPDATED OCCUPIERS CASES

Occupiers' Liability Act cases are possibly one of the most common types of slipping and tripping cases that the claimant lawyer will deal with. The claimant's solicitor will commonly find that these types of slipping and tripping accidents occur in supermarkets, shopping centres and other licensed premises where there is a risk from either tripping or slipping accidents.

This chapter will deal with slipping and tripping cases in relation to supermarkets, shopping centres and other licensed premises, on private land where the Occupiers' Liability Act 1957 is likely to apply. This chapter in particular will look at how to deal with these cases economically and efficiently and the ways in which these types of cases can be investigated particularly with references to fixed costs post-Jackson.

This chapter is aimed to be a quick reference guide for the majority of Occupiers' Liability 1957 Act cases. It should be borne in mind that Occupiers' Liability Act cases can encompass a large cross sector of potential accident scenarios that will not be covered by the scope of this chapter, but the chapter is designed to provide a starting point for the investigation into these types of cases.

The Duty Under The Occupiers' Liability Act 1957

The Occupiers' Liability Act 1957 sets out the duty of care required in relation to such cases and is as follows:-

"The common duty of care is a duty to take such care as in all the circumstances of the case is reasonable to see that the visitor will be reasonably safe in using the premises for the purpose for which she is invited or permitted by the occupier to be there".

In other words, in order for the claimant to recover damages under the Act the claimant must show breach of the common law duty of care.

Tripping Accidents

Often in practice, the claimant lawyer will come across a situation where a claimant has tripped over an item or a defect in the land on private land and often these cases will fall within the remit of the Occupiers' Liability Act 1957.

The starting point for the investigation in relation to such a case is to obtain photographs of the relevant defect that has caused the tripping accident. Contrary to popular misconception, there is generally no accepted level at which the Court will consider a defect becomes dangerous. Whether a defect is dangerous or not will depend upon all the circumstances of the case. For example, a defect which is in the middle of a car park there is going to be less of a duty upon the occupier to repair such a defect than for example a defect which is immediately outside the entrance to the store. Therefore one of the first investigations the claimant's solicitor should look at in such a case is where the defect was actually located. Often good quality photographs will be of assistance in this regard especially if a defect is in a prominent position where there is likely to be lots of footfall in that area.

It may be argued that it is important to encourage the claimant to take good quality photographs of the defect as soon as it occurs or as soon as possible after it happened. It will be particularly important to have good quality photographs measuring the defect with either a measuring implement, or if not available, other items inserted into the defect so reference can be made to the depth of it.

In relation to such cases for example, a defect in the tarmac outside a supermarket entrance, if the defendant denies that the defect was dangerous, one should ask the defendant for disclosure of the footfall into the supermarket for that day. This will provide a good indicator as to whether it was reasonable for it to be repaired in all the circumstances, and how quickly it should have been repaired.

When looking at tripping cases on private land, the claimant lawyer will also want to see maintenance and inspection records for the premises. Often large retail premises or other occupiers who have large footfall into their stores, will generally keep maintenance and inspection records for the property and have someone inspect it on a regular basis. The claimant will want to see those inspection records to see whether the defendant occupier has met their relevant obligations under the Act. When investigating a tripping claim, the claimant lawyer will also wish to obtain copies of any CCTV footage or other witness evidence and especially a copy of the accident report form to confirm what was recorded as to the mechanism of the accident.

Examples of slipping and tripping cases on private premises are as follows:-

Lydia Mary Searson –v- Brioland Limited 2005 EWCA Civ 55. The claimant in this case Mrs Searson was a lady who was 82 years of age at the time of the accident and had attended her granddaughter's wedding which was taking place in a suite of rooms slightly removed from the main premises of the hotel. The entrance to that part of the hotel required people to pass through two sets of doors, inner doors and external doors. The two sets of doors appear to have been of a similar construction but the outer doors were different in that they led onto the car park and there was an entrance to the doors and an up stand so described some 2.8cms above the flush level of the floor. They led to a step or steps which a person coming into the hotel would have to climb before entering the stairs. This entrance was not the main entrance to the hotel but it was regularly and frequently used by large numbers of people. Indeed it was part of the defendant's case that very large numbers of people pass through the doors since the hotel opened, but

Mrs Searson was the first one to suffer injury. Mrs Searson's evidence was accepted by the Judge that she wished to speak to the relatives of hers whom she had not seen for some time and whom she thought would find the car park already described and going out of the door she looked ahead in an attempt to see this person and tripped over the up stand suffering unfortunately quite a severe injury.

The Judge finding for the claimant said as follows:-

> *"So here is the claimant who in my Judgment has acted perfectly reasonably, perfectly normally with nothing to warn her of a possible projection in the floor impeding her access to the outside, who tripped over it and the only answer to her claim effectively is that she should have looked where she was going. But why should she have looked where she was going defeats me. It seems to me that there was no warning, no reason whatsoever why she would have expected something to be sticking up out of the floor on her way out".*

The defendant on appeal argued that there was no sound evidential basis concluding that the premises were not reasonably safe.

An appeal in that case was dismissed and the Court of Appeal made a finding essentially that:-

> *"Lord Justice May; I agree that this Appeal should be dismissed for the reasons which Buxton LJ has given. The point at which the claimant tripped and fell was a principal guest entrance, an exit to and from a much used hotel or Conference and Banqueting Centre. To a person going out of the premises there was as Buxton LJ has explained an up stand of rather more than an inch immediately followed by a step down four inches. The claimant tripped over the up stand. She did not expect to find a hazard such as this in a place such as this. This was evidently a case for a Judge to decide as a matter of broad general experience upon experience which in the absence of a technical case from the defendant really needed to go no further than some good photographs of the relevant dimensions. He concluded in effect that the up stand and I would add that the step down following*

it was without a clear warning a hazard to those approaching the door from inside the hotel".

The application of *Searson –v- Brioland* is a good illustration of how the Courts will interpret occupiers' liability cases with good common sense in the absence of a technical defence from the defendant. It is clear from *Searson* that the case was determined in favour of the claimant simply with reference to good quality photographs and the claimant's evidence.

In the case of *Bukardilicli –v- Hammerton UK Properties & Standard Life Assurance Companies 2002 EWCA Civ 683*, an accident occurred at Brent Cross Shopping Centre. There was a tarmac parking area at the edge of which is a raised pavement with an ordinary kerb at its edge. Set in at the outer part of the pavement was a roughly rectangular area of prepared soil. At its side it was almost flush with the top of the kerb and on the far side however as one went towards the shop door the soil was bounded by a line of slim kerbstone standing as the Judge found higher than the surface of the prepared soil. The Judge in the instant case having listened to the evidence found that the bit of kerb stood two inches proud of the soil. He also found that there was nothing to stop customers walking across the bed and there was no reason to suppose that someone would not do so. The issue in the appeal was firstly whether the claimant tripped at all and secondly, if she did trip whether the lip over which she tripped was too small to be a hazard for which the defendant was liable and thirdly, whether she was the author of her own misfortune for failure to look where she was going.

The Judge at the initial trial found:

> *"the claimant tripped over the lip which was about two inches above the top of the compacted earth and the top of the kerbstone. It is true that her husband was very vague as to his estimate of the measurement but his figure of between 5 and 7 cms is confirmed by the photographs themselves which although not very clear indicate a lip of about two inches. I accept that she caught her foot on this lip whilst walking forwards. This was the effective cause of her falling and breaking her leg. She also fell onto the kerbstone itself onto the other*

side. The kerbstone looks to be about some three to four inches high. I think the right analysis of the kerbstone was also causative of the accident but that the effect cause was the lip. --- the first and second defendants had known for many months that the public were in the habit of walking across the uncompleted rough flowerbed. Indeed the earth was compacted obviously by the feet of many walkers. I cannot quantify more precisely that many people over many months use the flowerbed as a pathway both to and from this store. The flowerbed was strategically placed right in front of those busy doors and this was the reason it was so frequently used.

The appearance of the flowerbed however made it clear that this was only a rough temporary structure. I have no doubt the claimant appreciated that it was not intended to be a finished access route. She may well have thought that it was intended to be a flowerbed in due course but it was quite obvious that it was a rough and temporary structure of some sort.

She could plainly see that the earth was rough and irregular. She could not plainly see that the rough earth was bounded by a para-meter of kerbstones on three sides that is to the north, south and east. On the west of course it was bounded by a concrete path. I accept her evidence that she did not see the lip, but she should have done. Knowing the structure was rough and temporary it behove to keep a careful look out as to the shape, confirmation and position of the boundary with the kerbstone."

The Judge in the first instance case found that the defendant was liable as occupiers of the area but reduced the figure awarded for damages by 75% for contributory negligence on the grounds that the kerb was there and she had simply not seen it and the defendant's appealed the Judge's findings on liability but the appeal was dismissed.

This again goes to highlight that occupiers' tripping cases are often determined by the court on pure common sense, looking at how dangerous the defect was in all the circumstances. Therefore it is important that one looks carefully at the outset of the case at the tripping hazard and in particular considers whether that tripping hazard will be a danger in light of all the circumstances.

One when investigating such a case will want to look at the lighting in the area where the accident took place, the layout of the locus, if the claimant has crossed what appears to be an unsafe area, whether there was another route around which would have avoided this, all the factors, in the circumstances.

The claimant lawyer will want to place themselves into such a position to ask the question on the balance of probability is the Judge likely to accept that the defect was dangerous in the area where the accident took place? The cases of *Searson* and *Bukardilicli* are illustrative of this fact.

Slipping and Tripping Cases in Supermarkets

The key case in relation to supermarket slipping and tripping cases is *Ward –v- Tesco Stores Limited 1976 1ER 219 SCA*. In this case the claimant slipped on some spilled yoghurt in a supermarket and on the evidence it was established that:-

• The defendant brushed the floor about half a dozen times a day.

• Any staff noticing a spillage were to call for its removal.

• Staff were to remain by the spill to guard against any accident in the interim.

The Court of Appeal held that the defendant had not had sufficient time to clear up the spill as they had not cleared it up and there had not been an adequate inspection process and accordingly the court held in the claimant's favour.

In slipping cases in supermarkets and other retail premises, the burden is on the defendant to show an adequate system of inspection is in place.

The claimant lawyer will find in practice that many larger retail premises will operate a clean as you go policy in relation to slipping cases in supermarkets. Therefore in order for the claimant lawyer to consider the reasonableness of the system of inspection, one will often need to see the following documents in practice:-

The cleaning and inspection logs usually operated by caretaker, cleaners or the like, to show when the area in which the claimant slipped was last inspected prior to the slipping accident. One should be particularly careful to look for evidence that the log has been filled in properly and any omissions in the log to show that the area in question was missed or not inspected properly.

If there is any doubt the claimant lawyer would often ask to see logs from the previous days or weeks to confirm whether the defendant's operatives had completed them correctly.

When assessing the reasonability of the system of cleaning or inspection, the claimant lawyer will want to obtain copies of the previous accidents or incidents, which have led to injury in the twelve months prior to the accident and the six months post-accident. If the defendant's system has had a large number of accidents or incidents leading to injury within a short period of time this may indicate that the system of inspection is not a reasonable one.

When looking at the defendant's system of cleaning and inspection, the claimant lawyer will wish to see the training records for the members of staff who were implementing the policy on the day of the accident. If the particular staff identified, haven't received correct training in the policy, then it may be argued that this is not an effective one.

If a slip or trip occurs in a supermarket, the claimant lawyer must look at the system of inspection and maintenance carefully in order to check that the exact area in which the claimant fell had been checked on a regular basis. Again the duty to look at to clean or inspect an area on a regular basis is likely to depend upon the number of people using that area of the defendant's premises at the time. For example, if the slipping incident occurs on an aisle in the supermarket where there are lots of liquids for example the laundry aisle where there are likely to be lots of boxes of liquids such as washing products etc. the duty to inspect that area may be higher than for example in a non liquids section of the supermarket where spillages are less likely to occur.

The defendant occupier of a supermarket in such a case should be asked for disclosure of the footfall into the supermarket on the day the accident took place and this can then be compared to the number of staff who are on duty on the date of the accident who were charged with the cleaning or inspection regime. If, for example, a large super-market has a very high footfall i.e. on a Saturday, then it may be argued that the duty to employ additional staff to undertake the system of cleaning and inspection will be higher when there are more customers in the store. Most supermarkets these days have the ability to electron-ically monitor the number of customers in the store on any particular day.

Very often supermarkets will argue that they have a clean as you go policy in place for all the staff that are employed on any particular day. This will often be argued in large fast food restaurants where somebody has slipped in such a premises. In such circumstances the claimant lawyer will want to ask for copies of all the staff training records for the staff that were on duty upon that day and in particular the area in which the claimant's accident took place.

One should always bear in mind that the duty is to take care as is reas-onable in all of the circumstances and whether the defendant occupier's system of cleaning and inspection is reasonable in all the circumstances will depend upon many of the factors listed above.

Some of the following cases are useful when applying *Ward –v- Tesco Stores Limited* in relation to systems of cleaning and inspection.

In the case of *Piccolo –v- Larkstock Limited & Chiltern Railway & Grew*

& Ebela & First Choice Cleaning Supplies Limited 1997 it was held that the owner of a flower shop on a station concourse had been responsible for the personal injury suffered by a claimant where he slipped and fell after slipping on a petal as it had negligently failed to operate a reasonable and effective system of work for dealing with the danger of falling petals.

In this case the Judge found:

> *"where there is a foreseeable risk of falling debris that may cause injury if walked on, I found that the risk that petals will fall in some sort of operation upon which the first defendants were engaged and the consequent risk of injury were not safeguarded against a purely reactive system in which steps were taken only when something was brought to the notice of the first defendant. It required a proactive system. I accept Mr Wilson's evidence that for substantial periods staff were not present in the shop front area and I found that the dropping of petals could occur inadvertently as with the spillage of water. I find that no-one had overall responsibility on a day to day basis for supervision and checking that the concourse was clear.*

> *It is not the claimant's case that the spillage should have been removed until it had fallen. However, I find that the system did not operate until a member of staff had become aware of the spillage was not an effective and reasonable system as I find the case was here, there was neither any member of staff with ongoing responsibility to check nor sufficient presence of staff outside the shop to ensure that the finding of removal of spillage very soon after it had fallen. By relying upon the acquisition of knowledge by the staff in the situation the system did not regulate or limit the amount of time that the spillage would have been on the floor before being seen. --- I find that the system of clean as you go without an element of a responsible person checking, and with staff remaining in the shop, was not a safe system of work. It was not reasonably effective and a safe system for dealing with the danger of fallen petals and I find that the first defendant did not have a safe system of work".*

The Judge went on to find that paragraph 47 of his Judgment:

> "I find that the elements of this case are in line with those in Ward – v- Tesco Stores Limited and that the reasoning in that case applies here to render the first defendant liable. I find that the type of accident that was sustained by the claimant is not one in the ordinary course of events does occur and that the first defendant has failed to establish that there was in place an effective and reasonable system for dealing with spillages. I find that this accident arose due to the breach of duty of the first defendant and I find that the first defendant had not shown that they had a safe system of work or that that system was implemented at the time".

In occupiers' slipping cases the claimant lawyer should also be careful to check whether there is an additional duty upon the defendant, for example when it had been raining at the time of the accident, for example if the claimant had slipped on water or the like that had been brought onto the occupiers' retail premises.

In such circumstances the claimant should ask the defendant occupier for disclosure of such documents as to the risk assessment and the defendant's procedures for what happens when it is raining outside the defendant premises. Often one will find that the risk assessment sets out that when it is raining the defendant should take extra steps such as putting a non slip matting at the entrance to the store, having the cleaning operatives undertake extra rounds within the premises when it is raining or putting out warning signs that the floor may be slippery. The claimant lawyer will in any event want to check that such actions were undertaken in the event that a claimant has slipped on water that is being brought in from the outside of the defendant store rather than slipping on the liquid or other substance within the store.

The claimant lawyer should also be careful to check that in relation to the system of inspection whether the liquid would have been visible to the store operative in any event, even if a reasonable system of inspection and cleaning had been in place. For example if the claimant tripped on a clear or opaque liquid, careful checks need to be undertaken as to whether any system would have spotted such a liquid or substance against the floor upon which the claimant slipped. If the liquid would not have been spotted in any event by the system of inspection then the defendant may not be in breach of duty. In such circumstances one should be careful to obtain if possible colour photographs of the liquid against the floor to see how visible it would have been to the defendant's cleaning operative.

Another useful slipping case in a supermarket is the Court of Appeal case of *Jacobs –v- Tesco Stores Limited*. In this case it was found that the Judge had been correct in finding the defendant company liable for the claimant's accident and that the company had failed to take all reasonable practical steps to keep the floor free from slippery substances. It was for the defendant to establish that they had done all that was reasonably practical to avoid the accident.

The circumstances of the accident were that on the evening of the accident Mrs Jacob was hurrying to answer a call and walked through one of the unmanned tills in the defendant's premises and in doing so trod on a small puddle of water which she had not previously noticed. She instructed the nearest cashier to stand by the spillage and call for a cleaner and then she continued to the spot where help was required and after some 25 paces she fell heavily on her buttocks and sustained injury.

The Judge found in the appeal case that:

> *"and what Tesco in calling such evidence is seeking to do is first to demonstrate that it did all reasonably practical to keep the floor free from spillages (i.e. that they had a proper system) or (as a fall back, that the accident in question would have at least equally likely to have happened despite a proper system designed to give reasonable protection to customers) as per Megaw LJ in Ward –v- Tesco Stores Limited (supra at 816d)".*

> *"Here Tesco call no evidence as to their accident record, no evidence as to any managerial input into their system. I simply report this I*

am not suggesting they should have. Instead they called some of those on the shop floor to explain the system. It was simple. The store was thoroughly clean before it opened in the morning. Then all employees had a second responsibility additional to their principal task, with a duty if they saw a spill to stand and watch over it until the cleaner came and made it safe. This simple system was taught in the employer's induction training of which no criticism was made. The Judge made no criticism of the system as it was and it worked after detection of the spillage. There were two cleaners on duty by day and one on the second shift they sat in the room until summonsed".

"The criticism that Mr Williams made of the system was that it was entirely reactive and unsupervised (all Indians and no chiefs). He suggested that there should be someone whose responsibility it was specifically to look out for spillages and also to ensure that all members of staff kept up to the mark in reporting and dealing with spillages be observed. But the weakness in the secondary responsibility scheme was that workers would be concentrating on the task for which they were primarily responsibile particularly in busy times".

The Court of Appeal found:

"In my Judgment this was just one of the sorts of spillages that would have been promptly and reliably detected by employers in the region – such employers e.g. the checkout assistant) that would have had their eyes elsewhere. Had there been a system of walked inspections, the spillage should have been detected earlier and had it been, Mrs Jacobs would not have slipped".

Summary

Therefore, when looking at an occupiers' slipping or tripping case, the system of inspection is going to be key in slipping cases in a supermarket or other retail premises.

As to whether the system is reasonable or not is always going to be subjective and it will depend upon whether the defendant can show a reasonable system in the first instance.

More often than not in practice, one commonly finds that the larger supermarkets are more easily able to show a system of inspection than the smaller retail premises. However, simply because there is a system in place does not always mean that the defendant occupier has adhered to that system. In practice the claimant's solicitor will always want to obtain evidence as to compliance with the system by those working under it starting from the cleaning operatives who are filling in the check lists and cleaning records to the staff members who are supervising the system.

The claimant lawyer will always want to obtain copies of the risk assessments that are put in place and copies of the defendant's policies to check that the defendant was adhering these to in practice. If not, this may lead to the court finding that a system of inspection was an unreasonable one.

In terms of tripping cases, evidence of the defect is always going to be necessary and measurements if possible are required. Whether a defect in the defendant's tarmac or the like is going to be enough to establish breach will depend upon where the defect is in relation to the number of customers walking over it and also how long the defect has been there for.

In either event, evidence as to other tripping or slipping accidents and a large number of concentrated accidents particularly before or post the claimant's accident is always going to be helpful in establishing breach of duty.

UPDATE 2018: McGeown v Northern Ireland

One of the defences often run in low value cases is known as a *McGeown* defence. This is the principle that a person using a public right of way is not owed a duty of care by the owner of the soil over which the right of way passes to maintain the right of way in a safe condition.

In order for *McGeowan* to apply the Defendant would have to show that has remained open and unobstructed use by the public for more than 20 years

Section 31 of the Highways Act 1980 sets out:-

31
Dedication of way as highway presumed after public use for 20 years.

(1) Where a way over any land, other than a way of such a character that use of it by the public could not give rise at common law to any presumption of dedication, has been actually enjoyed by the public as of right and without interruption for a full period of 20 years, the way is to be deemed to have been dedicated as a highway unless there is sufficient evidence that there was no intention during that period to dedicate it.

[F1(1A) Subsection (1)—

(a) is subject to section 66 of the Natural Environment and Rural Communities Act 2006 (dedication by virtue of use for mechanically propelled vehicles no longer possible), but

(b) applies in relation to the dedication of a restricted byway by virtue of use for non-mechanically propelled vehicles as it applies in relation to the dedication of any other description of highway which does not include a public right of way for mechanically propelled vehicles.]

(2) The period of 20 years referred to in subsection (1) above is to be calculated retrospectively from the date when the right of the public to use the way is brought into question, whether by a notice such as is mentioned in subsection (3) below or otherwise.

In the alternative, there is an argument that under Lowery v Walker [1911]AC10. If the Defendant knew that member had habitually used the land for a number of years, and the defendant took no steps to prevent this, this would create an implied licence through repeated trespass. Arguably if there was an implied licence *McGoewn v Northern Ireland* would not apply.

UPDATE 2018: Case Updates

Edwards v Sutton [2016] EWCA Civ 1005

An ornamental bridge in a local authority park, which crossed a stream with rocks in and had a low parapet presented, objectively, a danger from "the state of the premises" within the Occupiers' Liability Act 1957 s.1 such as to give rise to a common law duty of care. However, the danger was obvious to users, and occupiers were not duty-bound to protect against obvious dangers. A formal risk assessment would not have lessened the accident risk, and the provision of side barriers would not have been proportionate. The Judgment said: -

"Discussion and my conclusions

The claim was brought under the Occupiers' Liability Act 1957. The relevant provisions are sections 1(1) and 2(1), (2) and (3) the Act. They provide as follows:

"1. Preliminary

(1) The rules enacted by the two next following sections shall have effect, in place of the rules of the common law, to regulate the duty which an occupier of premises owes to his visitors in respect of dangers due to the state of the premises or to things done or omitted to be done on them...."

"2. Extent of occupier's ordinary duty

(1) An occupier of premises owes the same duty, the "common duty of care", to all his visitors, except in so far as he is free to and does extend, restrict, modify or exclude his duty to any visitor or visitors by agreement or otherwise.

(2) The common duty of care is a duty to take such care as in all the circumstances of the case is reasonable to see that the visitor will be reasonably safe in using the premises for the purposes for which he is invited or permitted by the occupier to be there.

(3) The circumstances relevant for the present purpose include the degree of care, and of want of care, which would ordinarily be looked for in such a visitor, so that (for example) in proper cases—

(a) an occupier must be prepared for children to be less careful than adults; and

(b) an occupier may expect that a person, in the exercise of his calling, will appreciate and guard against any special risks ordinarily incident to it, so far as the occupier leaves him free to do so...."

36. *The judge perceived there to be a contrast between those provisions and the parallel provisions of the Occupiers' Liability Act 1984 regulating the duties owed to persons other than visitors, i.e. principally trespassers. As noted above, the judge said (in the passage quoted above) that section 2 of the 1957 Act did not demand the safety of the premises as such but that the visitor be "safe in using the premises for the purpose for which he or she is invited or permitted by the occupier to be there". He contrasted this with the words of section 1(1) of the 1984 Act which provides as follows:*

"(1) The rules enacted by this section shall have effect, in place of the rules of the common law, to determine-

(a) whether any duty is owed by a person as occupier of premises to persons other than his visitors in respect of any risk of their suffering injury on the premises by reason of any danger due to the state of the

premises or to things done or omitted to be done on them; and

(b) if so, what that duty is."

37. *It seems to me, however, that the terms of section 1 of the 1957 Act and section 1(1) of the 1984 Act are not materially different in the relevant respects. Both Acts regulate the different duties imposed on an occupier, in respect of visitors and others, "[in respect of dangers/by reason of any danger] due to the state of the premises or things done or omitted to be done on them".*

38. *Thus, as it seems to me, it is necessary to identify what danger(s) there is/are before one can see to what (if anything) the occupier's duty in each case attaches. That that approach is necessary is clear from the speech of Lord Hobhouse in Tomlinson's case at paragraphs 69 to 70 and the speech of Lord Hoffmann at paragraph 29. For my part, I do not think that the judge focussed adequately on this issue. The case cited by the judge in paragraph 46 of the judgment: Hughes v Lord Advocate, was one in which there was a clear potential danger presented by the lighted lamp. It was, as Lord Reid put it, "a known source of danger" ([1963] AC at p.845).*

39. *Mr McDermott argued at our hearing that the danger presented in this case was "simple" and the judge did not have to be precise. However, when pressed further on the point by the court, he said that danger "due to the state of the premises" was the low parapets and the potential for a fall on to rocks. As for "things done" on the premises, Mr McDermott pointed to the actions of persons such as the claimant wheeling a bicycle as they are permitted to do. With regard to "things...omitted to be done" he relied upon the failure to provide guard rails.*

40. *Looking first at "things done or omitted to be done", I find it hard to see how this activity on Mr Edwards' own part, of walking with his bicycle over this bridge, constituted a danger for these purposes and the failure to provide guard rails seems to me to add nothing at*

all to whatever may be derived as a danger arising from the "state of the premises".

41. *Looking then at "the state of the premises", i.e. of the bridge, it is impossible to see how the third and fourth features identified by the judge in paragraph 43 of the judgment could be material: there was no suggestion that the "tarmac fillet", placed to rectify a tripping hazard, or the join between the bridge's surface and the pathway played any part in Mr Edwards' accident. That leaves, in effect, the acknowledgment by Mr Scandachanmugasran that the low parapet could be dangerous as the only feature of "danger" from the physical state of the bridge. In this regard, the expert witness, Mr Alford, said that the sides of the bridge were "effectively unguarded". Therefore, he saw no difference between a bridge with low parapets and a bridge with no side barriers at all, while the judge seems to have seen some additional peril from the potential for a pivot over a parapet, adding to the danger of a fall.* **Of course, whether the danger is such as to trigger the duty under the Act is a matter of evaluation for the court nonetheless.**

42. *One can see that an unfenced bridge or a bridge with low parapets will present more danger of a fall than would a bridge with high guard rails. There are, of course, many such unprotected bridges up and down the country in all sorts of locations. In argument, we discussed golf courses, where plank bridges, with no side rails, crossing over ditches are common and have to be negotiated by golfers with trolleys. Ornamental bridges with low walls, together with water features, are likely to be common features of decoration in public gardens. Any structure of this type presents the risk that the user may fall from it. Unlike natural land features, such as steep slopes or difficult terrain or cliffs close to coastal paths, which Lord Hobhouse in Tomlinson said could hardly be described as part of the "state of the premises", it seems to me that a bridge with no sides or only low ones may present a danger from the "state of the premises" such as to give rise to the common duty of care. However, while I am prepared to assume that there was objectively a "danger" arising from the state of the premises in this respect here, does this mean*

that, in order to discharge the common duty of care, arising from that objective possibility of danger, no such bridges must be left open to visitors or must not be left open to visitors without guard rails or express warnings? In my judgment, the answer to this question is a clear "no".

43. **The reason for this answer lies, I think, in two well recognised principles of law. First, there is the proper treatment in law of the concept of risk. Secondly, occupiers of land are not under a duty to protect, or even to warn, against obvious dangers. Both** these propositions appear in the speeches in Tomlinson's case.

44. The first proposition can be taken from the speech of Lord Hobhouse at paragraphs 79 and 80 as follows:

"79. To suffer a broken neck and paralysis for life could hardly be a more serious injury; any loss of life is a consequence of the greatest seriousness. There was undoubtedly a risk of drowning for inexperienced, incompetent or drunken swimmers in the deeper parts of the mere or in patches of weed when they were out of their depth although no lives had actually been lost. But there was no evidence of any incident where anyone before the claimant had broken his neck by plunging from a standing position and striking his head on the smooth sandy bottom on which he was standing... The park had been open to the public since about 1982. Some 160,000 people used to visit the park in a year. Up to 200 would be bathing in the mere on a fine summer's day. Yet the number of incidents involving the mere were so few. It is a fallacy to say that because drowning is a serious matter there is therefore a serious risk of drowning. In truth the risk of a drowning was very low indeed and there had never actually been one and the accident suffered by the claimant was unique. Whilst broken necks can result from incautious or reckless diving, the probability of one being suffered in the circumstances of the claimant were so remote that the risk was minimal. The internal reports before his accident make the common but elementary error of confusing the seriousness of the outcome with the degree of risk that it will occur.

*80. The third point is that this confusion leads to the erroneous con-
clusion that there was a significant risk of injury presented to the
claimant when he went into the shallow water on the day in question.
One cannot say that there was no risk of injury because we know now
what happened. But, in my view, it was objectively so small a risk as
not to trigger section 1(1) of the 1984 Act, otherwise every injury would
suffice because it must imply the existence of some risk. However, and
probably more importantly, the degree of risk is central to the assessment
of what reasonably should be expected of the occupier and what would
be a reasonable response to the existence of that degree of risk. The
response should be appropriate and proportionate to both the degree of
risk and the seriousness of the outcome at risk. If the risk of serious
injury is so slight and remote that it is highly unlikely ever to materi-
alise, it may well be that it is not reasonable to expect the occupier to
take any steps to protect anyone against it. The law does not require disproportionate or unreasonable responses."*

45. *A similar statement appears in the speech of Lord Oaksey in Bolton
v Stone [1951] AC 850, 863 as follows:*

**"The standard of care in the law of negligence is the standard of an
ordinary careful man, but in my opinion an ordinary careful man
does not take precautions against every foreseeable risk. He can, of
course, foresee the possibility of many risks, but life would be almost
impossible if he were to attempt to take precautions against every
risk which he can foresee. He takes precautions against risks which
are reasonably likely to happen. Many foreseeable risks are
extremely unlikely to happen and cannot be guarded against, except
by the most complete isolation."**

46. *Allied with the issue of foreseeability of likelihood risk is the balance
of risk, gravity of injury, cost and social value. As to this, I would
refer to paragraph 34 of Lord Hoffmann's speech in Tomlinson:*

*"The balance of risk, gravity of injury, cost and social value
34. My Lords, the majority of the Court of Appeal appear to have proceeded on the basis that if there was a foreseeable risk of serious injury,*

the council was under a duty to do what was necessary to prevent it. But this in my opinion is an over- simplification. **Even in the case of the duty owed to a lawful visitor under section 2(2) of the 1957 Act and even if the risk had been attributable to the state of the premises rather than the acts of Mr Tomlinson, the question of what amounts to "such care as in all the circumstances of the case is reasonable" depends upon assessing, as in the case of common law negligence, not only the likelihood that someone may be injured and the seriousness of the injury which may occur, but also the social value of the activity which gives rise to the risk and the cost of preventative measures. These factors have to be balanced against each other."**
While there are limits on social value in a case of this sort, the amenity of this bridge as a feature in the park should not be ignored entirely.

47. *The second proposition is, in my judgment, a particularly forceful consideration in this case. That there was some risk of a fall and the potential for injury must have been obvious. The approach to the bridge was clear and unobstructed. The width of the bridge and the height of the parapets were also obvious to the eye. The bridge was also over water, with whatever might lie beneath its surface. Any user of the bridge would appreciate the need to take care and any user limiting the width of the bridge's track, by pushing a bicycle to his side, would see the need to take extra care.*

48. *In my judgment, the present case is similar to Staples v W. Dorset DC [1995] PIQR 439. In that case, the defendant council was the "occupier" of the Cobb, a harbour wall at Lyme Regis to which the public had access as a promenade. The wall sloped downwards towards the sea. The surface had a tendency to slipperiness when wet. It had a drop of 20 feet to rocks on one side and one of 8 feet to a lower walkway on the other. The plaintiff, positioned some 3 feet from the edge, crouched to take a photograph, lost his footing and fell from the wall sustaining injury. There were no warning signs against a slippery surface. The judge held that there should have been. That decision was reversed on appeal. This court held that a warning would not have told the plaintiff anything that he did not know from his own observation; the most that could be said*

was that if there had been a notice the plaintiff might have behaved with more circumspection, but a bare possibility was not enough to establish causation in any event.

49. *It was common ground that the duty of care under the 1957 Act arose in that case. However, there was no liability for failure to warn. Kennedy LJ said:*

"It is, in my judgment, of significance that the duty is a duty owed by the occupier to the individual visitor, so that it can only be said that there was a duty to warn if without a warning the visitor in question would have been unaware of the nature and extent of the risk. As the statute makes clear, there may be circumstances in which even an explicit warning will not absolve the occupier from liability (see s.4(a) above); but if the danger is obvious, the visitor is able to appreciate it, he is not under any kind of pressure and he is free to do what is necessary for his own safety, then no warning is required. So, for example, it is unnecessary to warn an adult of sound mind that it is dangerous to go near the edge of an obvious cliff (see Cotton v. Derbyshire Dales District Council (June 10, 1994, C.A., unreported). *In the present case, as Mr Tyson for the respondent acknowledges, he must succeed under the Occupiers' Liability Act or fail, because, although the judge also referred to negligence at common law, there was no other relationship between these parties that could give rise to liability."*

Evans LJ added this:

"I find myself driven to the conclusion that the respondent cannot attribute negligence to the appellants in circumstances where nothing was known to them, or would have been known to them if previous inspections had been made, which he did not know and appreciate for himself. If the cause of his accident was the general state of the algae-covered strip at the seaward edge of the Cobb, combined with the pronounced 1:5 slope of the top, then the danger posed was obvious and in fact was appreciated by him. If the cause was an isolated slippery path, which had not manifested itself as a source of

potential danger during the 165-year history of the Cobb, then that was not something which the appellants should have foreseen, nor is it clear what the terms of a specific warning would have been. Whichever it was, the appellants cannot be held liable in negligence by reason of their failure to erect warning notices before his accident occurred."

Nourse LJ agreed with both judgments.

50. *The court also found that it was in as good a position to evaluate the question of liability as had been the trial judge; nothing turned on an assessment of witnesses. To my mind, the same is true here, having proper regard to the principles emerging from Re B (supra).*

51. *A notable feature of the Staples case was the absence of previous accidents, which was perhaps surprising given the nature of the structure, its location and its tendency to be slippery. The absence of accidents is an important feature in the case before us. There is no recorded accident of any character, let alone with the type of consequence that befell Mr Edwards. When weighing up the remarks of Lord Oaksey and of Lord Hobhouse (quoted above) in the context of this case, it appears to me that the probability of such an accident could properly have been sufficiently remote that the risk could be regarded as minimal.*

52. *That brings me to certain additional features of the case with which I should deal: a) the photograph, presented as potential fresh evidence; b) risk assessments (or their absence); c) the need (if any) to bring the bridge up to "modern" standards of protection for users.*

53. *On the first point, the photograph, I have considered its features very carefully. Out of a sense of overall justice to a severely injured claimant, we should, I believe, admit it formally into evidence. It is designed to show, as already mentioned, that the metalled footway leading to the bridge may not have been present in 1987, when the photograph was taken, and thus that the users of the bridge in earlier years may have been fewer than in more recent times.*

Accordingly, it is argued, the potential for accidents to have occurred may have been considerably less than contended for by Sutton.

54. *The photograph has its limitations. It is an aerial image taken from a significant height. The bridge itself and its immediate access is obscured by a tree. It does not show that access to the bridge was barred and we cannot know what facility for access there was. Equally, there is no doubt that there has been a path to the bridge for some time and no evidence suggested that it was a merely recent addition at the time of Mr Edwards' accident. Therefore, Sutton is entitled to say that the absence of recorded accidents is significant. I do not consider that the admission of the photograph into evidence alters the balance of argument to any significant extent for or against either party.*

55. *The judge took the view that the risk posed by the bridge should have been formally identified and assessed. He was influenced by the decision of this court in Uren v Corporate Leisure (UK) Ltd. and in particular the remarks of Smith LJ which I have quoted above. Mr Warnock pointed out all the cases (bar one) cited by Mr McDermott are decisions made in an employment law context where the employer's duty is to take positive thought for the safety of employees beyond that owed to the general public. The one exception was Corbett v Cumbria Kart Racing Club [2013] EWHC 1362 (QB) (King J), which involved the conduct of a hazardous activity, namely a karting race in which it could well be envisaged that there were risks to the safety of spectators and assessment of potential risk to them was obviously important.*

56. *Mr Warnock also submits that the court must ask what a formal risk assessment would have produced in this case. He relied upon comments of Floyd LJ in Nicholls v Ladbrokes Betting & Gaming Ltd. [2013] EWCA Civ 1963 where it is pointed out that without a finding of what a risk assessment would have produced, the absence of such an assessment does not help a claimant.*

57. *On the facts of this case likewise, I do not see what a formal assessment would have produced (if anything at all) beyond a statement of the obvious, namely that this was a bridge with low parapets over water; persons not exercising proper care might fall off. I do not see how such a statement would have led to steps being taken that would have prevented or lessened the possibility of Mr Edwards' accident occurring.*

58. *In resisting Mr Edwards' cross-appeal against the judge's finding that there was no obligation on Sutton to erect side barriers on the bridge, Mr Warnock relies heavily upon this court's decision in Japp v Virgin Holidays Ltd. [2013] PIQR 8 in which a holiday-maker sued a tour operator in respect of an injury suffered when she walked into a glass sliding door on a hotel balcony. It was argued for her that the glass in the door failed to meet contemporary standards requiring the use of safety glass in this type of building. The court held that in deciding whether a structural feature complies with local standards, the starting point had to be the standards applicable at the date of design and construction. I have quoted above the relevant passage from the judgment of Richards LJ, with whom Tomlinson LJ and my Lord, Lewison LJ agreed,*

59. *Mr Warnock submits that in this case there were no standards, concerning side- barriers, which were directly applicable to this bridge and that, therefore, there can be no requirement upon Sutton to update the structure so as to accord with the type of standard referred to by Mr Alford as being called for on modern bridges.*

60. *I agree that the existence of new standards for side barriers to be fitted to new and different structures cannot necessarily lead to a conclusion that an occupier is liable in negligence if an older structure does not meet those standards. I do not consider, however, that such an argument necessarily relieves an occupier of liability for breach of the common duty of care when an accident, for which a serious risk of occurrence exists, results from a dangerous state of premises which could readily be remedied by proportionate works of renovation. For the purposes of the present case nonetheless, it seems*

to me that there was no requirement to provide this bridge with the type of side barriers advocated on Mr Edwards' behalf. Such additions would have altered the character of the bridge significantly and to an extent out of proportion to a remote risk which had never materialised in its known history.

61. *Mr Edwards has suffered injury which can evoke nothing but the most enormous sympathy. However, in line with the authority which I have endeavoured to cite, I find myself in agreement with Mr Warnock's final submission in opening Sutton's appeal that not every accident (even if it has serious consequences) has to have been the fault of another; and an occupier is not an insurer against injuries sustained on his premises. In my judgment, like the court in Staples' case,* **I think that the standard was set too high by the judge below and I would allow this appeal and would dismiss the cross appeal**"

Key Points

1. It is necessary to identify what danger(s) there is/are before one can see to what (if anything) the occupier's duty in each case attaches.

2. Whether the danger is such as to trigger the duty under the Act is a matter of evaluation for the court.

3. The standard of care in the law of negligence is the standard of an ordinary careful man, and an ordinary careful man does not take precautions against every foreseeable risk.

4. If the danger is obvious, the visitor is able to appreciate it, he is not under any kind of pressure and he is free to do what is necessary for his own safety, then no warning is required. So, for example, it is unnecessary to warn an adult of sound mind that it is dangerous to go near the edge of an obvious cliff.

CHAPTER SIX
OCCUPIERS' LIABILITY SPECIAL CONSIDERATIONS, CHILDREN AND INDEPENDENT CONTRACTORS

When dealing with occupiers' liability cases, there are a number of important considerations and special circumstances to be taken into consideration when dealing with such cases. This chapter will look at the special considerations such as cases involving children and independent contractors, provide a summary of the cases in this area and special considerations to be given and for claimant solicitors when looking at such cases.

This directly links into the chapter of the book that deals with occupiers' liability cases in general.

Infants

Section 2 (3) of the Occupiers' Liability Act 1957 says as follows:-

"The circumstances relevant for the present purposes including the degree of care, and of want of care, which would ordinarily be looked for in such a visitor, so that for example in proper cases – (a) the occupier must be prepared for children to be less careful than adults and an occupier may expect that a person in the exercise of his calling will appreciate and guard against any special risk ordinarily incident to it so far as the occupiers leaves him free to do so".

Therefore the legislation clearly sets out that occupiers of private land must guard against the risks posed to children and to take this into account against potential risk.

The leading case in this is set out in *Phipps –v- Rochester Corporation 1955 1QB 540* where Lord Justice Devlin said:-

"It is their duty to see that such children are not allowed to wander about by themselves or at least to satisfy themselves that the places to which they do allow their children to go unaccompanied are safe for them to go to. It would not be socially desirable if parents were, as a matter of course, able to shift the burden of looking after their children from their own shoulders to those who happen to have accessible bits of land".

Therefore for claimant lawyers dealing with an injury to a child under an Occupiers' Liability 1957 case, the claimant's solicitor will want to see disclosure of the following documentation:-

- The risk assessments which show how the defendant guarded against risk to children or infants.

- Practical steps that the defendant have taken to guard against risks to children or infants i.e. in a supermarket case where somebody had cut themselves on a low shelf in the supermarket, had the supermarket guarded against the risk by making the shelf edges rounded to avoid injury to children.

The case that highlights the duty to children is found in *Young –v- Kent County Council 2005 EWCA 1342*. The court found that the council had failed in its duty of care to protect children from a known risk to them climbing on the roof of a school building and they have been in breach of that duty where a council had failed to protect against that risk despite a low cost solution.

Workers

Section 2 (3) (b) of the Occupiers' Liability Act 1957 says:-

"The circumstances relevant for the present purposes include the degree of care and for want of care which would ordinarily be looked for in such a visitor so that for example in proper cases – an occupier may expect that a person in the exercise of his calling will appreciate

and guard against any special risk ordinarily incident to it so far as the occupier leaves him free to do so".

This may mean for example that if an occupier employs a person to undertake work on the premises, then if those occupiers have a special skill or expertise, it is expected that the workers will guard against the risks arising out of their occupation.

Independent Contractors

Under the Occupiers' Liability Act 1957 Section 2 (4) (b) this states that in some circumstances, an occupier will not be liable for the damage created by an independent contractor and Section 2 (4)(b) of the Act sets out as follows:-

"Where damage is caused to a visitor by a danger due to a faulty execution of any work of construction, maintenance or repair by an independent contractor employed by an occupier, the occupier is not to be treated as more than answerable for the danger if in all the circumstances he has acted reasonably in entrusting the work to an independent contractor and had taken such steps if any as he reasonably ought to in order to satisfy himself that the contract was competent and that the work had been properly done".

Therefore it may be argued that the Act is designed to protect occupiers who had entrusted work to an independent contractor but the occupier in such circumstances has taken steps to make sure that the contractor was competent and the work had been properly done.

In other words the occupier cannot simply contract out to an independent contractor and this will avoid any liability under the Act.

This was well illustrated in the case of *Johnson –v- BJW Property Developments Limited 2002 EWCA TCC* where the Court found that the defendant was liable in both negligence and nuisance for damage caused by the claimant's property by fire that had escaped from the defendant's property due to the negligence of the defendant's contractor.

This was further illustrated in the case of *James Alexander Yates –v- National Trust 2014 EWCA 222 QB.* In this case, the claimant had employed a tree surgeon to cut down some trees. The work involved removing branches and then cutting down a trunk in sections. The claimant climbed the tree using a rope and harness and began to cut off the branches and he was working at a height of about 50 metres when he fell to the ground suffering a fracture to his spine. It was held in this case that although the defendant owed a duty to the claimant under the Occupiers Liability Act 1957 as a lawful visitor to its premises, this was not the relevant duty in the instant case. In any event, if the 1957 Act had applied, Section 23(b) would have been relevant because the defendant would not have been expected to guard against a risk ordinarily incident to the occupation of a tree surgeon who was climbing a tree with a chain saw.

What is an Occupier?

The reader will note that the 1957 Act provides no definition of an occupier, but the question was addressed in *Wheat –v- E Lacon* by Lord Denning and he said as follows in relation to the question of occupation:-

> *"In order for there to be an occupier it is not necessary for a person to have entire control over the premises. He need not have exclusive occupation. Suffice it is that he has some degree of control. He may share the control with others. Two or more may be occupiers. Whenever this happens each is under a duty to use care towards persons coming onto the premises, dependent on his degree of control. If each fails in his duty each is liable to the visitor who is injured in consequence of his failure but each may have a contribution from the other".*

Therefore, in order for a claimant to bring a claim against the occupier of the land, the claimant must show that the occupier had some degree of control over the land in question.

The Judgment in *Wheat –v- Lacon* makes it clear that there may be more than one occupier on the same premises, and in the circumstances when the claimant is investigating the case at the outset it will be important to establish who the occupier was of the land in question.

It may well be that there is a licensee over part of the premises, and where land is leased, generally speaking the occupier will part with all control of the land. It will usually therefore be necessary to obtain copies of any licences or leases over the property when investigating for example an accident that has happened where it appears that there is more than one occupier to the property, for example a concession stall on land at an event.

Normally where such instances arise, it will be necessary to obtain a copy of the lease or the licence to establish who had occupation or control of the land where the accident took place and therefore who is the correct defendant to sue under the Act.

The burden of proof will of course be on the claimant to show that the defendant was the occupier for the purpose of the 1957 Act.

Risks Willingly Accepted

Section 2 (5) of the Occupiers' Liability Act states:-

> *"The common duty of care does not impose on an occupier any oblig-ation to a visitor in respect of risks willingly accepted by the visitor (the question whether a risk was so accepted to be decided on the same principles as in other cases in which one owes a duty of care to another)".*

Therefore, if a danger has been willingly accepted by a visitor and therefore, there is unlikely to be breach of duty under the Act.

One commonly finds this arises in sporting injury type cases where claims are brought under the Occupiers' Liability Act.

For example in *Pinchbeck –v- Craggy Island Limited 2002*, a company that operated an indoor rock climbing centre was two thirds liable for injuries sustained by a climber who jumped down from a wall and injured her ankle as she had not been given appropriate instructions as to how to descend the wall but the climber was at some degree of fault and the maxim of Volenti Non Fit Injuria applied.

The Judge in that case said:-

> *"Mr Foster in accepting that the maxim applies to risks voluntary undertaken and nevertheless submits that it only applies to one which inevitably arise from the activity where all the appropriate care taken by those supervising and instructing to explain safety procedures. I have found in the instant case that all appropriate care had not been taken by those supervising and instructing to explain safety procedures. Had they done so the accident would probably not have occurred. If a participant has followed the appropriate instruction and training but nonetheless suffers a fall which may happen even though the appropriate precautions were taken the maxim may apply. Here the claimant's employers having paid for her to be trained the claimant consented to such inevitably uncontrolled risks (or, putting it in another way an unavoidable risk) as were involved but not a risk which could or should have been eliminated or avoided by proper instruction and supervision. This was one such".*

In the case of *Ruth Geary –v- J D Wetherspoon plc 2011 EWCA 150 6QB*, 29 March 2011 the claimant had been drinking with some work colleagues at a pub in Newcastle City Centre. One of the original features of the building, which was left untouched by a refurbishment, was a grand staircase in the centre of the building with sweeping bannisters on both sides rising to a half a landing and then turning upwards to either side on the first floor. On her way out with colleagues the claimant hoisted herself onto the left side bannister with the intention of sliding downwards but unfortunately she fell backwards and landed on a marble floor just less than four metres below sustaining a fracture to her spine.

The Judge found:

> "*in light of the Claimant's candid evidence about the risk that she ran it seems to me that the principle of voluntary assumption of risks set out in those cases is fatal to her claim. The claimant had freely chosen to do something which she knew to be dangerous. Because of the conversations about "Mary Poppins" there was even a degree of pre planning. She knew that sliding down the bannister was not permitted but she chose to do it anyway. She was therefore the author of her own misfortune. The Defendant owed no duty to protect her from such an obvious and inherent risk. She made a genuine informed choice and the risk that she chose to run materialised with tragic consequences. In those circumstances I consider on the Law I am bound to find that this claim must fail. It would be contrary to binding authority to do otherwise*".

Warnings & Exclusion of Liability

Section 2 (4) of the Occupiers' Liability Act 1957 says:-

> "*In determining whether the occupier of premises has discharged the common duty of care to the visitor regard is to be had to all the circumstances so that for example:-*
>
> *Where the damage is caused to a visitor by a danger which had been warned by the occupier, the warning is not to be treated without more than absolving the occupier from liability, unless it was in all the circumstances enough to enable the visitor to be reasonably safe.*
>
> *It is clear, therefore a warning on its own will not be enough to exclude liability.*"

This is helpfully highlighted in the case of *John Peter Tomlinson –v-*

Congleton Borough Council 2002 EWCA Civ 309. This featured a park and at the centre of it was a lake. It was an extremely popular venue where yachting, sub aqua diving and other regulated activities were permitted but swimming and diving were not and there was a prohibition made clear by notices reading dangerous water no swimming. On 6 May 1995 the claimant went there after work with some friends in the early afternoon and at one point in the afternoon the claimant dived from a standing position in the water which came no higher than his mid-thigh and the claimant struck his head with sufficient force to drive his fifth cervical vertebrae into his spinal canal which paralysed him from the neck down. With regards to warning notices the Court said:-

> *"In discharge of the common duty of care owed to visitors under the Occupiers' Liability Act 1957, the authority has placed prominent signs which forbade swimming and warned of the dangerous water. In entering the water against the prohibition the claimant made himself a trespasser to whom a different duty was now owed. If there was on the notice board no swimming qualified the use he was permitted to make of the facility do the words above or below that dangerous water constitute some protection against a risk of injury if a person were to take a swim? It may be too narrow a view of a warning notice which serves a composite purpose of turning a visitor into a trespasser and also warning him of the danger but this does not rest here. The misuse of the facility to the extent of the unauthorised swim in the history of accidents and the perceived risk of fatality were noted and acted upon by the occupiers over many years. They did not as may have been the fact in some of the undecided cases treat the notice as sufficient to discharge any duty that might be owed. Here the authority has employed rangers whose duty it was to give oral warnings against swimming albeit this met with mixed success and sometimes attracted abuse for their troubles. --- It seems to me that the rangers' patrols and advice and handing out of these leaflets reinforced the ineffective message on the site and constituted some protection in fact given unreasonably expected to be offered in the circumstances of the case --- in my Judgment the gravity of the risk of injury and frequency by which it was using the park came to be exposed to the risk the failure of the warning signs to curtail the*

extent to which the risk was being run indeed the very fact of the attractiveness of the beach and lake acted as a magnet to draw so many into the cooling waters, all this leads me to the conclusion that the occupiers were reasonably expected to offer some protection against the risk of entering the water".

Therefore, in this instance, the warning signs were not enough.

Summary & Conclusions

The reader will note that there are a number of provisions within the Occupiers' Liability Act 1957 when considering cases being brought under the Act. When considering any case under the Occupiers' Liability Act 1957, it is therefore always worth considering the point raised in this chapter in any case brought under the Act and in particular the special circumstances involving cases involving children, independent contractors, accidents that happen with the involvement of workers, warning signs present, or the other circumstances referred to in this chapter.

Early consideration of the issues will enable the claimant's lawyer to identify the issues in the case early on and identify any potential problems with the case under the Occupiers' Act at an early stage.

CHAPTER SEVEN
CLAIMS UNDER THE OCCUPIERS' LIABILITY ACT 1984 – UPDATED 2018 WITH NEW CASES

It is clear that the Occupiers' Liability Act 1957 has no application where there are trespassers on land as opposed to a visitor within the meaning of the 1957 Act. A visitor within the meaning of the 1957 Act is someone who is invited onto premises for a specific purpose or anyone who goes onto the premises with the express or implied permission of the occupier as opposed to someone who is not permitted to be on the premises and is thus a trespasser.

Therefore if there is a general invitation to members of the public i.e. retail premises or public buildings then anyone entering will be a visitor for the purpose of the 1957 Act.

However the 1957 Act will not extend to persons who are not lawfully entitled to be on the premises and therefore this is where the 1984 Act will apply since that person will become a trespasser.

Who Is Owed A Duty Of Care Under The 1984 Act?

The duty is owed to anyone not a visitor for the purpose of the 1957 Act for example someone using a private right of way may not be a trespasser but would be covered by the 1984 Act.

However persons using a right of way are not owed a duty of care under the 1984 Act by reason of Section 17.

What Is The Duty Of Care Owed Under the Act?

Section 1 of the Act provides that:-

"The rules enacted by this section shall have effect in the place of the rules of common to determine:-

Whether any duty is owed by a person who is occupying a premises to persons other than visitors in respect of any risk of their suffering injury on the premises by reason of a danger duty to the state of the premises or things done or omitted to be done by them; and

If so, what that duty is.

For the purpose of this Section the persons who are to be treated respectively as an occupier of any premises (which for those purposes, includes fixed or moveable structures and his visitors are (a) any person who owes in relation to the premises the duty referred to in Section 2 of the Occupiers' Liability Act 1957 (the common duty of care) and (b) those who are visitors for the purpose of that Act".

Section 3 goes on to say:-

"An occupier of the premises owes a duty to another not being a visitor in respect of any risk as is inferred into subsection 1 above.

If he is aware of the danger or has reasonable grounds to believe that it exists;

He knows or has reasonable grounds to believe that the other is in the vicinity of the danger concerned or that he may come into the vicinity of the danger (in either case whether the other has lawful authority for being in that vicinity or not); and

The risk is one against which in all the circumstances of the case he may reasonably be expected to offer the other some protection".

Section 4:-

"Whether by virtue of this section an occupier of premises owes a duty to another in respect of such a risk the duty is to take care as is reasonable in all the circumstances to see that he does not suffer injury on the premises by reason of the danger concerned".

Section 5:-

"Any duty owed by virtue of this section in respect of a risk may in an appropriate case be discharged by taking such steps that are reasonable in all the circumstances of the case and to give warning of the danger concerned or to discourage other persons from incurring the risk".

Section 6:-

"No duty is owed by virtue of this section in respect of risk willingly accepted by that person, the question whether a risk was so accepted to be decided on the same principles as in other cases in which one person owes a duty of care to another".

No duty is owed by virtue of this section to persons using the highway and this section shall not affect any duty owed to such persons".

Therefore, one can see under the Act that the duty is set out in the Occupiers' Liability Act 1957, very much mirrors the ones set out in the Occupiers' Liability Act 1957.

When Is The Duty Of Care Owed?

In *Keown –v- Coventry Healthcare NHS Trust in the Court of Appeal 2006* the grounds of River House were used not only as means of transit between surrounding streets but as a place where children liked to hang around, relax and play. The fire escape with cross bars on it outside were climbable and thus an attraction to adventurous children.

The claimant had seen other boys climb the fire escape in this way and on 8 October 1995 he decided to show his sister and his friends how this could be done and he fell from a height of about 30 feet fracturing his arm and suffering a significant brain injury which led to the loss of intelligence functioning.

In his evidence the claimant has said that he appreciated that it was dangerous to climb the underside of the fire escape and he knew that he should not be doing so. In his Judgment, the trial Judge found as follows:-

- There existed a danger due to the state of the premises.

- The Trust was aware of the circumstances giving rise to the danger and thus was aware of the danger.

- The Trust knew that children playing in the grounds and there was a risk of their coming into the vicinity of the fire escape.

- The risk of suffering injury by reason of the danger due to the state of the premises was a risk against which the Trust might reasonably be expected to offer some protection. This was because any fall from a considerable height <u>would be dangerous</u> and the cost of averting the risk by providing barriers, notices or security guards was not great.

- There was no express or implied agreement on the part of the claimant to be exempt from the Trust from liability as to attract the maximum of Volenti Non Fit Injuria.

In light of those finding the recorder decided that the Trust was in breach of the duty to Mr Keown and held that the claimant should himself carry the considerable proportion of blame and be two thirds responsible. The Trust appealed against this. The Court of Appeal dismissed the claim under the 1984 Act and found that neither the buildings nor the fire escapes themselves were dangerous and they were only made dangerous by the claimant's actions and in the case of children there was a duty to protect against the obvious risk that a child might not be able to recognise the danger that an adult might.

The Court of Appeal found that the claimant had known that there was a risk of falling and that what he was doing was dangerous and thus the risk arose not out of the state of the premises but out of what the claimant chose to do and consequently the defendant did not owe any duty to the claimant and even if it had done it would probably not have been in breach because there was not really anything he could reasonably have done to offer any protection against the risk.

In the case of *John Simon Donoghue –v- Folkestone Properties Limited 2003 EWCA Civ 231* the Court found that the Defendant, Harbour-master owed no duty of care to the claimant who was injured when he dived into the harbour after midnight in December. The Court of Appeal said that where a duty of care existed had to be determined with regards to the circumstances prevailing at the time when it was alleged that the breach of duty resulted in injury to the claimant.

The case of *Young –v- Kent County Council 2005 EWCA 1342* the Council was found liable under the 1984 Act. The claimant was playing football outside a youth club with other children. The football was kicked or thrown by one of the children onto the roof of the school building and the claimant climbed on to the flat roof to retrieve it. Whilst the claimant was on the roof of the building he fell through one of the skylights to the ground causing him serious personal injury.

In this case the Court posed four questions in its Judgment and made findings of fact on the following:-

> "1. *Did the state of the premises in this case pose a danger. Answer: Yes it did. The roof was an inherently dangerous place for a child particularly having regard to the brittle nature of the skylight. The state of the premises did pose a risk in the sense that children could fall off or be hurt by going through the skylight.*
>
> 2. *Is the danger one that poses a risk of causing injury to a non*

visitor. Answer: Yes. Had the claimant not been a child but rather an adult then he would have recovered nothing.

3.   Were there reasonable grounds for believing that the non visitor would come into the vicinity of the danger? Answer: On the evidence, plainly yes. They congregated there and this was known to be a meeting place.

4.   Are trespassing children, who had lawfully come into the school grounds but knowingly strayed from the part that they were allowed to be in entitled any protection from the defendant? Were the defendant under any obligation to protect the children from the consequences of their own mischievous behaviour? I take the view that the claimant would have known that he was misbehaving when he went onto the roof, although he had reason for being up there. He was retrieving a ball and not simply going on the roof for fun although I am sure that children who went onto the roof normally did so because it was fun as Ms Jones explains in her evidence. He would have known that this was a place that was forbidden to him. He would have been aware of the notices that the club roof warning the children of it. Once he was on the roof he would have known that it was not appropriate and it would be regarded as an act of vandalism if he were to step on, jump on or break the skylight. I cannot rule out the possibility that he missed his footing and fell but for reasons already explained on the balance of probability I think it is more likely that he jumped onto the skylight. He would have known that it was dangerous although he would have probably been unaware of the fragility of the skylight and would have jumped on it as he noted danger. Although he was rightly described as complicated with a hearing and learning disability I do not think that this provides any satisfactory explanation for his behaviour.

The school also would or should have known that if there was a roof to climb children will likely to climb it. The school would have known that access to the roof could be readily denied by the erection of two short fences at either end of the passageway with a gate in one to permit authorised access. This was a low cost solution to a danger which was, or should have been apparent to them. Thus the danger of serious injury to a child albeit a trespasser was or should have been apparent to the school and the prevention of the accident was cheap. In my view any school such as this ought to have carried out a risk assessment of their premises and if they have done so they would have come to the conclusion that there was a risk to children getting onto the roof and suffering injury or death and their failure to fence off the access point was negligent. Having invited children onto their property they did owe a duty to ensure that the wandering child, a non visitor or the trespasser was not allowed to encounter this danger. In my Judgment the defendant was in breach of their duty under the 1984 Act".

The majority of the reported cases in relation to Judgment for the claimant under the 1984 Act largely appear in relation to children and where there has been a foreseeable danger that children could stray onto the occupiers' property and those risks have not been guarded against.

When dealing with the claims under the 1984 Act, i.e. for trespassers or non visitors, it will therefore be important for the claimant's lawyer to consider the following matters in summary:-

Can the claimant prove the risk was one against which in all the circumstances of the case the occupier may have reasonably been expected to offer some protection? If not, then it is arguable that the claim is likely to fail.

It seems that cases where children are involved and the occupier has failed to guard against obvious risks are more likely to succeed.

UPDATE 2018: Occupiers Act 1984 Cases

SLAWOMIR KOLASA v EALING HOSPITAL NHS TRUST (2015) - A hospital trust did not owe a duty of care under the 1984 Act to an intoxicated patient who had discharged himself and sustained injuries after climbing over a wall on a ramp outside the hospital and falling 30 feet to the ground. The danger of the drop was obvious at all times, the wall was of sufficient height and maintenance, and the trust was not obliged to provide further protection. The Judgment said:-

36. *Before I turn to the legal principles which govern this case and the submissions of learned counsel I should indicate that in this case I am not considering any duty of care which might be argued to have been owed to the Claimant by the Defendant as a patient brought to the hospital in an ambulance. He had voluntarily discharged himself from A&E and, rightly, Particulars of Negligence and/or Breach of Statutory Duty (g) to (j) inclusive were struck out of the Particulars of Claim, leaving this a claim purely under the Occupiers' Liability Acts, to which duties the pleading of negligence adds nothing.*

42. *I also make the finding of fact that, although when the Claimant was brought to the hospital and was put to wait in A&E he was a visitor to the hospital and was owed the common duty of care under section 2(2) of the 1957 Act, his act of climbing over the wall was not an act covered by his general permission to be on the site as a patient nor was it part of the permission given by the Defendant to patients leaving the site after, or even without, treatment. He was, therefore, no longer an invitee or visitor but a trespasser.*

43. **To use the famous example of Lord Justice Scrutton in The Calgarth [1927] P 93 at page 110:**

   "When you invite a person into your house to use the staircase, you do not invite him to slide down the banisters – you invite him to use the staircase in the ordinary way in which it is used."

44. **Mr. Norris' primary submission to me is that the protection extended both to visitors and to trespassers under the 1957 and 1984 Acts respectively is from danger caused by the state of the premises, an "occupancy duty" rather than a more general obligation to protect the visitor/trespasser from danger he may face while on the premises. That is clear from the discussion of the law**

at paragraph 12-04 of the current edition of Clerk and Lindsell on Torts. I accept that submission.

45. **The most helpful authority which has been cited to me is the Court of Appeal decision in Keown v Coventry Healthcare NHS Trust [2006] 1 WLR 953.** *That case establishes or re-establishes the principle I have just referred to. The Claimant in that case was an 11 year old child who climbed the underside of an external metal fire escape of an accommodation block and day clinic in the grounds of a hospital owned by the Defendant trust and fell from a height of about 30 feet severely injuring himself. There was evidence in that case that the hospital grounds were known as a place where children liked to play. The claim was brought under the 1984 Act on the basis that the fire escape constituted a material danger and allurement to children. The Claimant accepted he appreciated that climbing the underside of the fire escape was dangerous and that he should not be doing it. The first instance judge found the occupier Defendant one third to blame for the accident as they were aware that children might come on to the staircase. The headnote sufficiently summarises the ratio of the case:*

"Held, allowing the appeal, that the threshold requirement posed by section 1(1)(a) of the Occupiers' Liability Act 1984 was not whether there was a risk of suffering injury by reason of the state of the premises, but whether there was a risk of injury by reason of any danger due to the state of the premises; that a fire escape was not inherently dangerous, so that, if a person chose to create danger by climbing it improperly knowing that it was dangerous to do so, any danger was due to such person's activity and not the state of the premises; that, in general, the age of the trespasser was not relevant, but it was a question of fact and degree whether premises which were not dangerous from the point of view of an adult could be dangerous for a child; that the Claimant had been aware not only that there was a risk of falling but also that his actions were dangerous and he should not have been climbing the exterior of the fire escape; and that, accordingly, no risk arose out of the state of the fire escape there being no element of disrepair or structural deficiency"

46. *While every case turns on its own facts, the Claimant's case here is actually far weaker than that of the Claimant in Keown.* **In my judgment, there was nothing dangerous about the state of the premises where the Claimant fell.** *The wall was of an adequate, safe height. It was no lower than walls at the sides of bridges or piers. The provision of an additional rail after Mr Talbot's accident was the reaction of a risk averse Defendant to the circumstances of his particular accident, which involved someone sitting on a part of the first floor perimeter wall in an area known to be used for recreational purposes, and, thus, falling to his death. The Defendant acted on the specific recommendation of the Safetymark report that the additional railing would deter people sitting on the wall. In my judgment, they could not have been criticised for not erecting the rail. The risk of falling when sitting on the wall was very obvious, whether by day or night. Neither rail nor warning signs were necessary to alert adults or even children to the risk. The report does not evidence that the wall and drop should have been protected or that they were unsafe. They were not. What was unsafe was the activity of sitting on the wall, an activity that Mr Krajewski had sensibly warned several people about prior to Mr Kolasa's accident.*

47. *However, that warning or even the knowledge which I find it can be inferred that the Defendant had of people sitting on the wall, does not evidence that the wall and drop represented an inherent danger either visitors or trespassers. It was not a hidden trap. It was easily visible and the danger of the drop obvious by day or night. It was not in a position in which it presented a danger. It was not in a defective state. It did not need guarding.*

48. *In any event, the railing which the Defendant erected after Mr Talbot's accident, and because of that accident and the report's recommendations, was erected to deter sitting on the wall and not climbing over the wall. The railing would not have prevented what the Claimant did, namely to climb over the wall. What was dangerous was not the state of the premises but what the Claimant, an*

adult, who had voluntarily consumed far too much alcohol and who was drunk, actually did. In truth, this accident was nothing to do with the state of the premises and was, instead, the entire fault of the Claimant, sad though it is to say that, given his very serious injuries.

49. *In many ways that decides the case against the Claimant, but in deference to the arguments of both counsel I should consider other legal issues.*

50. *In the absence of a supervisory duty to the Claimant, as a person who had been attending the hospital for treatment but had discharged himself before he could be seen, and having regard to the deletion of particulars based on a supervisory duty, it matters not that the Defendant could have expected that people who might be drunk and even those who might be in a shocked or upset state due to injury, might be present in or around A&E. The Defendant had not accepted, nor was it under, any duty to take particular care of a drunken adult. There is no satisfactory evidence that the Claimant was in fact suffering from the continuing effects of a head injury, even though there is some very slight evidence he had been concussed.*

51. ***It should be noted that, if the Claimant had been a visitor, section 2 (2) of the 1957 Act imposed on the Defendant a duty to take such care as in all the circumstances of the case was reasonable to see that he would be reasonably safe for the purposes for which he was invited or permitted by the occupier to be there.*** *Those purposes did not include climbing over the wall and I am wholly satisfied that the Defendant did discharge that duty if the Claimant was a visitor.*

52. *However, as I have found above, he was not a visitor at the time of the accident, he was a trespasser because he had gone further than his implied invitation and had tried to climb the wall.* ***Thus I have to consider the 1984 Act. The relevant provisions of the Act are as follows:***

"(1) The rules enacted by this section shall have effect, in place of the rules of the common law, to determine—

(a) whether any duty is owed by a person as occupier of premises to persons other than his visitors in respect of any risk of their suffering injury on the premises by reason of any danger due to the state of the premises or to things done or omitted to be done on them; and

(b) if so, what that duty is...............

(3) An occupier of premises owes a duty to another (not being his visitor) in respect of any such risk as is referred to in subsection (1) above if—

(a) he is aware of the danger or has reasonable grounds to believe that it exists;

(b) he knows or has reasonable grounds to believe that the other is in the vicinity of the danger concerned or that he may come into the vicinity of the danger (in either case, whether the other has lawful authority for being in that vicinity or not); and

(c) the risk is one against which, in all the circumstances of the case, he may reasonably be expected to offer the other some protection.

(4) Where, by virtue of this section, an occupier of premises owes a duty to another in respect of such a risk, the duty is to take such care as is reasonable in all the circumstances of the case to see that he does not suffer injury on the premises by reason of the danger concerned.

(5) Any duty owed by virtue of this section in respect of a risk may, in an appropriate case, be discharged by taking such steps as are reasonable in all the circumstances of the case to give warning of the danger concerned or to discourage persons from incurring

the risk.

(6) No duty is owed by virtue of this section to any person in respect of risks willingly accepted as his by that person (the question whether a risk was so accepted to be decided on the same principles as in other cases in which one person owes a duty of care to another)."

53. **Applying those provisions sequentially, as I have already determined, there was no danger due to the state of the premises and there was nothing done or omitted to be done in relation to the wall that made it dangerous.**

54. *Although the Defendant was aware of people climbing on to the perimeter wall and sitting on it, that was not the risk presented in this accident. Mr Levene submitted that I should not be too "nit picking" in relation to the designation or description of the "risk" presented and known to the Defendant, but the risk of someone climbing over the wall was of an entirely different nature and the Defendant was not and had no reason to be aware of the existence of that risk.*

55. *That remains the case, in my judgment, despite the fact that subsequent to the Claimant's accident the Defendant erected the metal rails.* **In Tomlinson v Congleton Borough Council and another [2002] EWCA Civ 309, the Defendant was aware of an increased risk of an accident from the unauthorised use of the lake** *and had begun work on a plan to landscape the shores and plant over the beaches from which people swam. That action did not evidence that the premises were not reasonably safe under the 1984 or 1957 Acts before the work was started.*

56. *In any event, if climbing over the wall and/or falling from it were the risks concerned and there had been evidence that the Defendant either was aware of them (which it was not) or had reasonable grounds to believe that they existed (which they did not),* **then they were not risks against which, in all the circumstances of the case,**

*it might reasonably be expected to offer the Claimant some
additional protection. I accept Mr Levene's submission that A&E
departments do have drunken people attending them and people
with head injuries, but in all the circumstances no further protection than the wall itself, which was of an adequate height,
needed to be provided. It was entirely reasonable for the Defendant
to have concentrated on the risk actually known to them when it
was brought to their attention, namely, the sitting on the wall by
certain visitors.*

57. *Thus, in my judgment, the Claimant has not established that the
Defendant owed him a duty of care under the 1984 Act in relation
to the risk of his climbing over the wall and falling to the area
below. If he had established that they did then I would have con-
cluded that they had taken such care as was reasonable in all the
circumstances to see he did not suffer injury on the premises by
reason of the danger presented by wall and drop. **It would have
been going further than was reasonable to raise the height of the
wall or put a rail or some other deterrent on top of the wall and
it would not have been effective in this case.***

58. **There was no need to give a warning because the risk was
obvious.**

59. *Finally, although the Claimant was drunk and had sustained some
head or facial injury that evening, I am satisfied he willingly
accepted the risk of climbing over the wall, though of course it was
something he would not have done had he been sober. Thus by
reason of section 1 (6) no duty would be owed by the Defendant to
him.*

60. *It seems to me to be quite obvious that, at the time of the accident,
the Claimant was a trespasser or, phrasing it alternatively, was no
longer a visitor acting within the scope of his permission but, if I
were wrong about that, **then I am entirely satisfied that the
Defendant had discharged the common duty of care to the
Claimant under section 2(2) of the 1957 Act by building and***

maintaining a perimeter wall of sufficient height and adequately lighting the area around the A&E.

61. *Mr Norris also argues that the deliberate actions of the Claimant were the entire cause of the accident. As I have already indicated, I consider that is entirely correct and the Claimant would fail on that basis as well. That seems to me a more appropriate way of putting the matter than to say that this is a case where the Claimant is 100% contributorily negligent.*

62. *For the reasons I have given, therefore, I dismiss the Claimant's claim.*

Key Points

1. The protection extended both to visitors and to trespassers under the 1957 and 1984 Acts respectively is from danger caused by the state of the premises, an "occupancy duty" rather than a more general obligation to protect the visitor/trespasser from danger he may face while on the premises.

2. In order to establish breach- there must be something dangerous about the area in which the claimant was injured.

3. There is no need to provide a warning if the risk was obvious.

4. There needs to be danger due to the state of the premises and / or something that was done or omitted in relation to make it dangerous.

5. There need to be a risk against which, in all the circumstances of the case, it might reasonably be expected to offer the Claimant some additional protection.

6. In *Tomlinson v Congleton Borough Council* and another [2002] EWCA Civ 309, the Defendant was aware of an increased risk of an accident from the unauthorised use of the lake.

CHAPTER EIGHT
HIGHWAYS ACT CLAIMS: THE LAW, IMPORTANT CASES AND SECTION 58 DEFENCES – UPDATED 2018 WITH NEW CASES

Highways Act cases under the Highways Act 1980 are probably some of the most common tripping cases whether they involve accidents on the road or on the pavement.

They are common types of claims for most claimant practitioners yet it may be argued probably some of the most misunderstood.

This chapter will deal predominantly with Highways Act tripping claims due to defects in the road or pavements. The chapter will look at relevant case law and defeating section 58 defences brought by the local authority.

The Law

Section 41 of the Highways Act 1980 sets out:-

> *"A duty to maintain highways maintainable at the public expense.*
>
> *The authority who are at the time being the highway authority for a highway maintainable at the public expense are under a duty subject to subsection 2 and 4 to maintain the highway.*
>
> *In particular a highway authority are under a duty to ensure that so far as is reasonably practical, the safe passage along the highway is not endangered by snow or ice".*

Section 328 of the Act defines the meaning of highway and defines it as:

"except where the context otherwise requires highway means the whole or part of the highway other than a ferry or water way. --- Where a highway passes over a bridge or through a tunnel, that bridge or tunnel is to be taken for the purpose of the Act as to be part of the highway. In this Act the highway maintainable at the public expense and any other expression defined by reference to a highway is to be construed in accordance with the foregoing provisions of this section".

For the purpose of claimant practitioners, a highway within the meaning of the Act is likely to be a carriageway or footway, more commonly referred to within claims as a road or a street.

Selecting the Correct Defendant

For the purpose of a Highways Act claim, or any other slipping and tripping claim which has occurred on the highway, it would be the claimant lawyer's first step to ensure that the correct defendant has been selected. The claimant's lawyer must ensure in the first instance that the land where the accident occurred is maintainable at the public expense.

If there is any dispute over this, it will often assist if the claimant's lawyer first of all writes to the highway authority concerned in order to check whether where the accident happened occurred on land maintainable at the public expense. It is always helpful at the outset of the claim to have the claimant draw on an ordnance survey map exactly where the accident took place and send this to the Council or local authority so the relevant local authority can make the checks to see if it is an adopted highway.

Local authorities are required to keep records of all roads which have been adopted and thus maintainable at the public expense so if there is any uncertainty the claimant can always ask for a copy of the relevant records from the local authority in order to make checks. At times there will be confusion on some parts of the highway, for example where private property meets the highway whether the accident occurred on the highway or private land and thus likely to fall as an Occupiers' Liability 1957 claim as opposed to a Highways Act claim.

However, again the relevant ordnance survey maps and disclosure from the Council as to whether the land is adopted or not will usually provide the answer to the question. It is therefore important to have clarity from the claimants to exactly where the accident occurred and who owns the land where the accident occurred.

With the advent of modern technology it is often easy now for the claimant's solicitor to go onto Google maps and to obtain photographs of the area in which the accident took place and again to ask the claimant to mark on the photographs exactly where the accident took place which can assist with identification as to whether where the accident took place forms part of the highway or not.

Breach of Duty Section 41 of the Highways Act 1980

In the context of a tripping claim, which are the most common types of claims under the Highways Act 1980, the claimant will have to show breach of Section 41 of the Highways Act 1980 in order to establish a claim against the defendant local authority.

This will usually mean showing that there was a relevant or actionable defect in the highway which caused the claimant to trip or fall. A common misconception in relation to highway tripping claims is that a defect of about an inch would be sufficient to establish a breach of duty on behalf of the local authority. In fact this is not correct and the level of the defect will be relevant to a number of factors including:-

Whether the defect was reasonably foreseeable that it would cause somebody to trip over.

It could be argued that a defect of one inch is likely to be found to be unsafe but it depends upon the nature of the highway and the persons using it.

The claimant will have to prove that the part of the highway in which the accident took place was not reasonably safe and therefore the injury was caused as a result of the defect.

It is well highlighted in the case of *Lorraine Flynn –v- Leeds City Council 2004*. The case found that a local authority was not liable for an injury suffered by a person as a result of a tripping accident on an uneven paving stone as she had failed to prove that the discrepancy between the paving stones was dangerous.

The claim arose out of a tripping accident on the afternoon of 23 August 2003 outside a row of shops on a public footpath on Lidget Lane in Leeds. The claimant at the material time had parked her car on the carriageway near to the bus stop and she was walking across the footpath before descending the steps to the lower flagged area carrying in front of her some dry cleaning because she needed to go to the launderette. She reached a point that was marked in the photographs with a 50p piece and the evidence established that one of her feet caught in a trip and she fell forwards and sustained a soft tissue injury to her foot and ankle.

The Judge found in that case:

> *"each case turns on its own facts and looking at the discrepancy and bearing in mind in one's daily experiences of footpaths I do not think it can be properly categorised as dangerous and probably why anybody fell over it and more relevantly nobody complained about it. ..... But even if I was wrong about that it was not generally perceived to be a source of danger".*

It was similarly emphasised in the case of *Joan Margaret Mills –v- Barnsley Metropolitan Borough Council 1992*. This case was a tripping claim and the Court held that a minor defect in the highway did not constitute a dangerous condition such that the highway authority was in breach of its duty to maintain. The test of dangerousness was one of foreseeable foresight of harm to users of the highway and each case would turn on its own facts.

The facts of this case were that on 1 March 1989 Mrs Mills was involved in an accident on Market Street in Barnsley. She was walking arm in arm with her husband along Market Street towards The Co-operative premises when she tripped and she sustained a strained ankle and fracture of the lower end of her tibia. The accident happened at a place where the corner of the paving bricks had broken away and the heel of the claimant's shoes became caught in a gap created by the missing corner.

The Judge in the case on appeal said:

> "like the Judge I do not consider that it would be right to say that a depression of less than one inch will never be dangerous but one inch will always be dangerous. Such action is not to be encouraged. Although one can say that the test of dangerousness is one of reasonable foresight of harm to users of the highway and each case will turn on its own facts. ---- In my judgement the photographs reveal a wholly unremarkable scene. Indeed it could be said that the layout of the slabs and the paving bricks appear to be excellent and that the missing corner of the brick is less significant than the irregularities and depressions which are a feature in streets in towns and cities up and down the country. In the same way as the public must expect a minor obstruction on roads such as cobblestones, cats' eyes and pedestrian crossings and so forth the public must expect minor depressions. Not surprisingly there was no evidence of any other tripping incident at a particular place although thousands of pedestrians probably passed on that part of the pavement while the corner of the brick was missing. Nor is there any evidence of any complaint before or after the incident about that part of the pavement. Like Mr Booth I regard the missing corner of the paving brick as a minor defect. The fact that Mrs Mills' fall must either have been caused by her inattention whilst passing over the uneven surface or by misfortune for present purposes it does not matter what precisely the cause is".

He went on to say:

> "it is important that our tort law should not impose unreasonably

high standards otherwise the scale of resources would be diverted away from situations where maintenance and repairs of the highway is urgently needed. This branch of the law of tort ought to represent a sensible balance of compromise between private and public interest. The Judge's ruling in this case if allowed to stand would tilt the balance too far in favour of the woman who was unfortunately injured in this case. The risk was of a low order and cost of rem- edying such minor defects all over the country would be enormous".

It is therefore important for Practitioners when dealing with cases under Section 41 of the Highways Act are to bear in mind the following con- siderations when looking at whether a defect is likely to be actionable under the Act or not:-

The defect in terms of height, length and width. There must be careful measurements of the defect taken as soon after the accident as possible with clear colour photographs of the defect.

The persons likely to be passing over the defect i.e. is it in the middle of the road or in the middle of the pavement or towards the side of the pavement where pedestrians are not likely to pass over it.

Strictly speaking, it may be argued, that any defect of less than an inch may struggle to meet the balance of probability test as a dangerous defect. However, this has to be taken on the individual facts of every case and in particular with reference to whereabouts in the highway the defect has occurred. If it has occurred in an area with particularly high footfall and pedestrian traffic, then it may be regarded as more dan- gerous and in breach of Section 41 of the Highways Act than a defect that appears in the middle of a country lane with very little traffic or pedestrians.

What Is The Duty To Maintain?

In *Haydon –v- Kent County Council 1973 1ALL ER 294* it was said that the ordinary duty to maintain was to:

"keep something in existence and in a state that may elicit to serve the purpose for which it exists. In the case of a highway that purpose is to provide a means of passage for pedestrians or vehicles or both (according to the character of the highway) to keep that purpose intact involved more than repairing or keeping in repair".

It is settled law that there is no duty upon a highway authority to improve the highway.

Section 58 Defences

Section 58 of the Act sets out as follows:-

"In an action against a highway authority in respect of damage resulting from a failure to maintain a highway maintainable at the public expense it is a defence without prejudice to any other defence or the application of law relating to contributory negligence) to prove that the highway authority had taken such care as in all the circumstances was reasonably required to secure that part of the highway for which the accident relates was not dangerous for traffic".

"For the purpose of a defence under subsection 1 above, the Court shall in particular have regard to the following matters:-

- *The character of the highway and the traffic that was reasonably expected to use it.*

- *The standard of maintenance appropriate for a highway of that character and used by such traffic.*

- *The state of repair in which a reasonable person would have expected to have found the highway.*

- *Whether the highway authority knew or could reasonably be expected to know that that part of the condition of the highway for which the accident relates was likely to cause danger to users of the highway.*

- *Whether the highway authority could have reasonably been expected to repair that part of the highway before the cause of action arose without warning notices if its condition is to be displayed.*

But for the purpose of such a defence it is not relevant to prove that the highway authority had arranged for a competent person to carry out or supervise the maintenance of the part of the highway to which the action relates unless it is also proved that the highway authority had given proper instructions with regards to the maintenance of the highway and that he had carried out those instructions".

Taking this into account, one will commonly find in practice that the local authority in almost all tripping claims will raise a section 58 defence at the outset in order to challenge the claim, save as to the most obvious defects, where there has been no system of inspection.

It may be argued, that the key for the claimant to succeed in claims under the Act is to defeat this section 58 defence.

The section 58 defence is normally defeated with reference to the matters set out in Section 58 paragraph 28(e) of the Highways Act 1980 and in particular showing that the defendant's system of inspection was unreasonable and each of the items is taken in turn.

The Character Of The Highway And The Traffic, Which Was Reasonably Expected To Use It

This section of the Act, is related to the nature of the road and the type of traffic that was passing over it. Thus for example where there is a very busy highway with lots of traffic passing over it, such as heavy goods vehicles and the like, it may be argued that there is a higher duty for a more regular system of inspection where for example heavy traffic is likely to cause deterioration to the highway. For example this may also be relevant as to whether a more regular system of inspection should be expected of a town centre road with lots of pedestrians passing over an area within a very short time as compared to a rural road with little or no traffic passing over it.

The argument may also be relevant to accidents involving pedal cycles and cycle lanes and it is an argument that the council and local authorities should take this into account when determining their system of inspection and maintenance.

This argument also largely takes into account the standard of maintenance appropriate for a highway of that character and used by such traffic and the arguments largely fall into the same bracket. In order to make arguments that the system of inspection was unreasonable the claimant may wish to adduce the following evidence:-

Evidence showing the volume of traffic which was passing over the highway on a regular basis. This may include witnesses who can attest to the type of traffic used on the highway, maps showing for example if a highway or area in which the claimant fell is close to a school or other large centres of population and therefore there are likely to have been lots of people using that section of the highway and/or video footage or the like, showing the type of traffic using that particular highway on that particular day and around that particular time.

As part of any disclosure order, the claimant will want to seek specific disclosure of the highway authority's inspection regime for the borough and the reasoning behind the inspection regime for that part of the highway. For example, in the case of *Jacobs –v- Hampshire Council 1984 The Times* where a road was particularly susceptible to water penetration, six months inspections were inadequate.

The State Of Repair In Which The Reasonable Person Would Have Expected To Have Found The Highway

This section of the Act relates to reasonable foreseeability of danger and the standard upon which a reasonable person would expect to have found the highway in such circumstances. Largely this criteria relates back to breach of duty and to some extent crosses over with the duty under Section 41 of the Highways Act 1980.

Whether The Highway Authority Knew Or Could Reasonably Been Expected To Know That That Condition Of The Part Of The Highway To Which The Action Relates Was Likely To Cause A Danger To Users Of The Highway

It may be argued, that in many tripping cases on the highway what is going to be key is whether the highway authority could reasonably have been expected to know that the condition of the highway was likely to be dangerous.

In practice, the claimant therefore may wish to make the following investigations in relation to any section 58 defence that the defendant local authority puts forward in relation to whether the authority could reasonably been expected to know or did know about the condition of the highway:-

The local authority should provide disclosure of systems of inspection, previous complaints about the highway in question, or previous inspection reports.

In particular the claimant's lawyer should be careful to check the defendant's disclosure about previous reports prior to the accident (at least 12 months before) as to whether there have been any previous complaints about that section of the highway, which should be enough in most circumstances if there were previous complaints about a particular pothole or defect to show that the defendant had constructive or actual knowledge of the defect and therefore it should have been repaired before the accident took place.

The claimant's solicitor will also want to look at map images that have been often taken in the past by the Google company, to see if the defect appears on Google street maps, prior to the claimant's slipping and tripping accident. If the defect appears previously on Google photographs, an opinion may be sought from an expert, as to the likely condition of the defect at the time of the defendant's last inspection, if the photographs were taken some time ago.

The defendant's previous inspection reports for at least twelve months before the accident, should be checked carefully to check whether the defect had been noticed or listed on a previous inspection by the local authority, and then simply had not been repaired or omitted.

The local authority's defence under section 58 will be that the defect was noted at the time of the last inspection, but one should be careful to check the manner in which the inspection was conducted and the claimant should ask the local authority:-

- Who conducted the inspection in question?

- What were the inspector's qualifications?

- Was it a walked or drive by inspection?

- If it was a drive by inspection and the pothole was at the side of the road, were there any parked cars on the side of the road and were checks made in relation to under the parked vehicles?

- How long did the inspection take?

One finds that when these questions are asked they sometimes come back with surprising results as to the manner in which the inspection took place. The inspection report in saying that the defect was not noted at the time of the last inspection should not be taken at face value by the claimant's solicitors and further questions should always be posted to the local authority about the manner and methodology by which the inspection took place.

The claimant can also ask for the highway inspectors' training records and also a copy of the guidance notes provided to the highways inspector as to what they are to look for on inspections and what they are to take account of.

Ultimately if the claimant can show that the highway authority knew or could reasonably have been expected to know as to the defect at the time of the last inspection, this will ordinarily strike a nail through the heart of the section 58 defence.

If the accident has happened on a residential road or outside shops, one will always wish to instruct an investigator to visit the shops or make enquiries with the local houses next to where the accident has taken place, in order to establish with the local residents how long the defect had been there and whether it would have been there at the time of the defendant's last inspection. However in order to obtain credible evidence, it will be necessary to obtain detailed witness statements from any of those witness statements to confirm the approximate measurements of the defect at the time of the last inspection.

Finally, any other accidents that had been caused by the same defect in the past, or a number of defects within a short period of time, are likely to be of assistance to the claimant under Section 58(2)(d).

Another relevant consideration is whether the highway authority knew that that part of the road was in a poor condition, even if they did not know about the defect which caused the accident.

For example if there are a number of significant defects on the same road, and the defendant has employed a lax system of inspection i.e. on a 12 month basis when there is an argument to say it should be on a six month basis because the number of defects at a particular accident location, an argument can be made that because of the number of defects on a particular road there should have been a more regular system of inspection. In a way this ties into the criteria under Section 58(2)(a) and 58(2)(b) of the 1980 Act.

If the rest of the highway was in a particularly poor condition, the claimant will want to obtain photographic evidence or video evidence of the number of other defects on the road, their locations, and particulars of the other defects.

Section 58(2)(e) of the Act also largely ties in to the same point and that is where the highway authority could have reasonably been expected to repair that part of the highway before the cause of action arose and what warning notices of its condition should have been displayed.

In the course of serious defects warning notices will be expected. This was highlighted in the case of *Morris –v- Thyssen GB* but unreported. If it can be shown that the highway authority knew or could reasonably have been expected to know that part of the condition to which the accident relates was likely to cause a danger to other road users, then the arguments that the highway authority could have reasonably repaired that part of the highway before the cause of action arose, is a reasonable one. However, of course, how quickly the highway authority should have repaired the defect is subjective and will to some extent it may be argued largely depend upon how dangerous the defect was in the road in all the circumstances.

Conclusions

The claimant lawyer should also bear in mind that there are a number of potential challenges to highways section 58 defences and the burden will always be upon the defendant local authority or highway authority to make out the section 58 defence.

A section 58 defence it may be argued should not be taken at face value and there are nearly always challenges that can be made to the section 58 defence. Very few section 58 defences are robust enough to evade challenge completely. One must consider a section 58 defence taken as a whole and whether a Court would find it reasonable in all the circumstances. In *Pridham –v– Hemel Hempstead Corporation 1970 114 SJ 884* it was held that if the authority can establish that its system of inspection is reasonable and that a fault occurred without its knowledge the authority will be discharged from its duty under section 58.

It is therefore one of reasonableness and if the inspection regime was reasonable and of course it had been carried out then the defendant will have made out the statutory defence.

It will be for the claimant therefore in challenging section 58 defences, to show with reference to the above matters that the system of inspection with reference to section 58(a) to (e) that it was an unreasonable one on the evidence.

UPDATE 2018: Highways Act 1980 Cases

PAUL SINGH v CITY OF CARDIFF COUNCIL (2017) looked at a claim both under the Highways Act section 41 and Occupiers Act section 2. The accident had not been caused by a breach of a duty under the Highways Act 1980 s.41, the Occupiers' Liability Act 1957 s.2 or breach of a common law duty.

The Court said went through the key principles of a Highways Act claim and said:-

1. *This is a claim for damages arising out of an incident on land between Fishguard Road and Trenchard Drive, Llanishen in Cardiff. The claimant, Mr Paul Singh, was walking home in the early hours of 10 December 2011 along a path that lead to a footbridge over Llanishen Brook. At some stage, he ceased to be on the path and went down into Llanishen Brook. He remained in the brook overnight and was found the following morning. He sustained severe injuries. He claims that the injuries were caused (1) by a breach of a duty owed by the defendant, Cardiff City Council,*

under section 41 of the Highways Act 1980 ("the 1980 Act") to maintain the footpath (2) a breach of the duty owed by the defendant under section 2 of the Occupier's Liability Act 1957 ("the 1957 Act") or (3) common law negligence on the part of the defendant. The defendant denies liability.

THE FIRST ISSUE – THE 1980 ACT

30 Mr Jones, on behalf of the claimant, submits that this footpath is a highway maintainable at public expense and this is accepted by the defendant. Mr Jones submits that the unevenness of the surface of the footpath and the irregularity of the concrete edging units gave rise to an state of disrepair and so as to amount to an actionable defect which, he submitted, caused the claimant to slip off the path and led to his injuries.

The Legal Framework

31 Section 41 of the 1980 Act provides, so far as material, as that:

"41.— Duty to maintain highways maintainable at public expense.

"(1) The authority who are for the time being the highway authority for a highway maintainable at the public expense are under a duty, subject to subsections (2) and (4) below, to maintain the highway.

Judgment Approved by the court for handing down. Singh v City of Cardiff Council

"(1A) In particular, a highway authority are under a duty to ensure, so far as is reasonably practicable, that safe passage along a highway is not endangered by snow or ice."

32 Section 329 of the 1980 Act provides that:

""maintenance" includes repair, and "maintain" and "maintainable" are to be construed accordingly".

33 Section 58 of the provides for a special defence. That section provides that:

"58.— Special defence in action against a highway authority for damages for non- repair of highway.

"(1) In an action against a highway authority in respect of damage resulting from their failure to maintain a highway maintainable at the public expense it is a defence (without prejudice to any other defence or the application of the law relating to contributory negligence) to prove that the authority had taken such care as in all the circumstances was reasonably required to secure that the part of the highway to which the action relates was not dangerous for traffic.

"(2) For the purposes of a defence under subsection (1) above, the court shall in particular have regard to the following matters:—

(a) the character of the highway, and the traffic which was reasonably to be expected to use it;

(b) the standard of maintenance appropriate for a highway of that character and used by such traffic;

(c) the state of repair in which a reasonable person would have expected to find the highway;

(d) whether the highway authority knew, or could reasonably have been expected to know, that the condition of the part of the highway to which the action relates was likely to cause danger to users of the highway;

(e) where the highway authority could not reasonably have been expected to repair that part of the highway before the cause of action arose, what warning notices of its condition had been displayed;

but for the purposes of such a defence it is not relevant to prove that the highway authority had arranged for a competent person to carry out or supervise the maintenance of the part of the highway to which the action relates unless it is also proved that the authority had given him proper instructions with regard to the maintenance of the highway and that he had carried out the instructions."

*34 **The claimant must establish that there is a breach and that that breach caused injury of a type which the statute intended to prevent.** If he does that, the defendant will have a defence to the claim if it can establish the defence established in section 58 of the 1980 Act.*

35 In terms of the scope of the duty imposed by section 41 of the 1980 Act, the Court of Appeal held in Jones v Rhondda Cynon Taff CBC [2008] EWCA Civ 1497, [2990] R.T.R. 13 at paragraph 11 that it is an absolute duty in the sense that:

Judgment Approved by the court for handing down. Singh v City of Cardiff Council

"the highway has to be maintained in a state of repair that it is reasonably passable for the ordinary traffic of the neighbourhood without danger caused by its physical condition".

36 In James v Preseli Pembrokeshire District Council [1999] P.I.Q.R. 114, Lloyd L.J. held that:

"The question in each case is whether the particular spot where the plaintiff tripped or fell was dangerous. If it was, then the defendant authority concedes that there was a failure to maintain the highway and the plaintiff would be entitled to recover. But if the particular spot was not dangerous, then it is irrelevant that there were other spots nearby that were dangerous or that the area as a whole was due for resurfacing.

"This point was made crystal-clear by the decision of this court in Whitworth v. The Mayor, Aldermen and Burgesses of The City of Manchester

. In that case the decision in favour of the plaintiff had been founded on the ground that the pavement as a whole was in poor condition. The Court of Appeal rejected that approach. Russell L.J. said at page 6 of the transcript dated June 17, 1971: "The relevant question is whether that which caused the accident constituted a danger, not whether nearby differences in levels which did not contribute to the accident constituted a danger."

"Edmund Davies L.J. said at page 7:

*"What is quite clear is that **when a plaintiff in a trip case claims that she fell by reason of the dangerous condition of the pavement, she must indicate where and how she fell and she must prove it; and it is then for the court to consider whether the place where she fell constituted a danger for which the local authority could properly be held liable.**"*

37. Ralph Gibson L.J, who agreed with Lloyd L.J., observed that:

"it has been established by the decisions of this court that the standard of care imposed by the law upon highway authorities is not to remove or repair all and any defects arising from failure to maintain, such as differences in level or gaps between paving stones, which might foreseeably cause a person using the carriageway or footpath to fall and suffer injury, but only those which are properly to be characterised as causing danger to pedestrians. There is, I think, an apparent element of circularity in some of the formulations of duty or breach of duty which have been advanced. Thus the test of dangerousness is one of reasonable foresight of harm to users of the highway. But in drawing the inference of dangerousness the court must not set too high a standard. Any defect, if its uncorrected presence is to impose a liability, must therefore be such that failure to repair shows a breach of duty. The escape from any apparent circularity was stated, or restated, I think, by Steyn L.J. in Mills v Barnsley Metropolitan Borough Council [1992] P.I.Q.R. P291 (to which my Lord has already referred) where, in holding that no breach of duty had been established, he pointed to the fact that the risk of injury from the

demonstrated defect was of a low order and that the fall suffered by the claimant in that case must have been caused by her inattention when passing over an uneven surface or by misfortune. "

The Present Case

38. *First, and foremost, in the present case, in my judgment, any alleged defect in the highway did not, in fact, cause the injury that the claimant suffered. As I have found above, the claimant did not trip over the concrete edging units of the footpath nor did he slip on the depression in the footpath. He voluntarily stepped off the footpath onto the ground adjacent to, but not part of, the highway. He lost his footing on that ground and fell on to his back and then slid down the steep slope and into the brook. His claim for breach of the duty imposed by the 1980 Act fails, therefore, because the injury suffered was not caused by any alleged defect in the footpath.*

39. *Secondly, and separately, I have considered whether the footpath at the location where the incident occurred was in a state of disrepair such as to amount to an actionable defect for the purposes of section 41 of the 1980 Act. I bear in mind that this footpath is approximately two metres wide. It has a metalled surface. It is well used as a means of going from one housing estate to another. It is used hundreds of times a day, and thousands of times a week, by people crossing over the brook.*

40. *The first defect identified and relied upon by the claimant is the broken and uneven edging units (there is an edging unit missing but that unit is missing near the bridge itself and not where the incident occurred). I find that the broken and uneven edging units are not such as to amount to a state of disrepair giving rise to a breach of the duty imposed by section 41 of the 1980 Act. The footpath is wide. There is ample room for persons to pass, and repass, over the footbridge without stepping on the concrete edging units. The risk of anyone tripping over the edging units at that point on the footpath and falling down into the brook is very low.*

41. *That view is reinforced by the expert evidence. Mr Hopwood for the defendant gave evidence that the primary purpose of the edging units would be to support the footpath and they would not expect to be walked on. The footpath was wide enough to be used without there being any need to step on the edging units and to allow people to pass each other. Mr Runacres for the claimant did identify this as a defect. He was, however, primarily concerned in his evidence, in my judgment, with the risk arising at a later point on the footpath, namely the risk that if someone left the footpath they could fall over the wing wall or the retaining wall and have a vertical drop into the brook. He was concerned that persons could stumble and fall, or there was a risk of inadvertent access to the area where the walls were and where there would be a steep fall into the brook. He was less concerned with the risk posed by the edging units further back from the bridge where a person, if they stumbled on that edging unit, would stumble and fall onto soil. He considered that gave rise to a reduced risk. In my judgment, the broken and uneven edging units in the vicinity where the incident occurred were not in such a state of disrepair as to give rise to a breach of the section 41 duty.*

42. *The second defect identified is the depression caused, probably by the support subsiding and the surface of the footpath becoming uneven. This was described as a depression and was measured by Mr Hopwood as being a depression of 60 millimetres (although it is likely to have been less at the time of the incident). I accept the accuracy of his measurement. This matter is of more concern. It occurs on a well used metalled footpath used many hundreds of times a day. The evidence of Mr Hopwood is that any depression of over 40 millimetres would be a matter of concern, although he would regard it as low risk.*

43. *On balance, I am satisfied that the depression did not amount to a defect or state of disrepair such as to cause a danger to pedestrians and its non-repair did not amount to a breach of section 41 of the 1980 Act. I accept that this is a busy footpath used many times a day. The depression, however, was not a pothole or a hazard capable of tripping someone. It was a change in height over*

an area to the left of the footpath. In terms of the location and the risk if a person did fall or slip from the path due to the depression, the person would fall onto soil adjacent to the area of the footpath containing the depression. There was no risk that the depression would cause someone to fall or stumble in such a way as to cause that person to fall over the wing wall or the retaining wall and endure a vertical drop into the brook. The risk posed by the depression was, therefore, relatively low as Mr Hopwood said.

44. *On balance, therefore, I consider that the presence of this depression on the footpath did not constitute a breach of the section 41 duty. I am reinforced in that conclusion by the fact that there is no record of any accident having occurred at this location over the time it is likely that a depression of something in the region of the size of this depression would have been present on the footpath. The claimant and Mr and Ms Donnelly who lived on the estates had used the footpath many times and not suffered an injury or had any cause to complain about the state of the footpath (Mr and Ms Donnelly had complained about the lights not working). The defendant provided the disclosure sought of complaints for three months from 1st October 2011 to 29 December 2011 and no complaints were recorded. Ms Bolwell made a witness statement stating that there had never been any complaints about the footbridge or the footpath before. Ms Bolwell was not well enough to give evidence and her evidence was not therefore tested in cross-examination. All the evidence is, however, that persons used the footpath hundreds of times a day when the depression was present and there was no recorded accident (still less a serious accident of the kind suffered by the claimant) and no recorded complaints. My conclusion that there is no breach of the section 41 duty is not dependent on the absence of recorded accidents or complaints: but it reinforces the conclusion that I have reached.*

45. *For completeness, I mention the evidence of certain of the other witnesses. Mr Rowlands, a lands service officer at the parks department of the defendant, carried out a survey of a section of Llanishen Brook on 23 November 2011, shortly before the incident. He sur-*

veyed the brook from the Rugby Club to the footbridge. He marked the condition of the bridge as 2 on a scale of 1 to 5, 1 being poor and 5 being good. He explained in evidence that he based that remark on the appearance of the bridge, graffiti and the presence of a shopping trolley. He was not, he said, expressing a view on the safety of the footbridge. He also marked the condition of footways and walkways and marked that as 2. He explained that that comment related to the whole section that he was surveying not specifically the footpath by the bridge. I found Mr Rowlands to be an honest witness and I accept his evidence about the survey document as truthful. He also gave his opinion about what he saw. He said he saw no obvious defect. I do not rely upon his opinion as to the state of the footpath. He was not familiar with this area. Furthermore, he is not a highways inspector but is a land services officer in the parks department, and has limited training in inspection. Whilst I accept that he genuinely did not consider there were any obvious defects in the footpath calling for any remediable work, his opinion on whether there was a defect did not assist me in reaching my conclusion.

46. Mr Misbah is a highway claims officer employed by the defendant and had previously been a highways officer. I did not find his evidence of assistance and he was an unsatisfactory and unreliable witness. He had not visited the site and his views were based on the photographs taken at the time although he admitted that it was not possible to gauge measurements from photographs alone. Furthermore, he was insistent that the footpath was the responsibility of the parks department not the highways department but displayed no understanding of how or why this footpath was in fact a highway maintainable at public expense.

Ms Mullane also gave evidence. Ms Mullane was the police officer who was responsible for the investigation into the incident. She had in fact been a community policer officer in the 1980s and early 1990s in Llanishen and had used the footpath and the bridge many times. She had never complained about the state of the footpath or the bridge. She expressed her view, however, that when she visited the site again in about December 2011 she thought the area was dark and dangerous. Her view was based on the fact that the footbridge had been designed in a way in which in her view the railings were not long enough and there was a significant drop on either side of the footpath. Ms Mullane is not, however, an expert in engineering or highways and had no background in engineering. She expressed her view as a person visiting the scene. Furthermore, her view was based on the area not on any observed defect in the footpath itself.

As I find that there was no breach of duty, it is not necessary to consider the defence under section 58 of the 1980 Act. I would note that the defendant does not identify the facts on which it relies in its defence. Its evidence on this issue was unclear and inchoate. The defendant's witnesses did not explain clearly why this footpath was left to the responsibility of the parks department and not inspected by the highways department in accordance with any relevant policy on inspections of footpaths even though the defendant accepted that it was a highway maintainable at public expense. **The defendant did not provide clear evidence as to what policy would have applied if it had been treated as a highway although a document was produced which referred to inspections of adopted footpaths being carried out on a reactive basis, that is in response to a complaint. No witness from the defendant in fact identified that document as containing the current, applicable policy to inspections of footpaths.** If I had found that there was an actionable defect which had caused the injury, I would not have found on the evidence before me that the defendant had established the defence in section 58 of the 1980 Act. I would not have been able on the evidence adduced by the defendant to find that it had taken such care as in all the circumstances (including those referred to in section 58(2)) was reasonably required to secure that the relevant part of the highway was not dangerous. In particular, if there had been a defect, I am not able to tell whether the defendant knew, or could have been expected to know, the condition of the highway given the absence of evidence about the applicable inspection regime for this footpath and, indeed, the evidence, that the footpath was *not inspected by the highways department of the defendant and was only considered as part of the parks services.*

Key Points

1. The question in each case is whether the particular spot where the claimant tripped or fell was dangerous. If it was, then the defendant authority concedes that there was a failure to maintain the highway and the claimant would be entitled to recover. But if the particular spot was not dangerous, then it is irrelevant that there were other spots nearby that were dangerous or that the area as a whole was due for resurfacing.

2. When a claimant in a trip case claims that she fell by reason of the dangerous condition of the pavement, she must indicate where and how she fell and she must prove it; and it is then for the court to consider whether the place where she fell constituted a danger for which the local authority could properly be held liable.

3. Thus the test of dangerousness is one of reasonable foresight of harm to users of the highway. But in drawing the inference of dangerousness the court must not set too high a standard. Any defect, if its uncorrected presence is to impose a liability, must therefore be such that failure to repair shows a breach of duty.

CHAPTER NINE
PUBLIC NUISANCE AND OTHER MISCELLANEOUS PROVISIONS: HOW THEY CAN ASSIST WITH HIGHWAYS CASES, THE LAW, CASE SUMMARIES AND PRACTICAL APPLICATIONS

The following chapter is predominantly designed to deal with nuisance but will also look at other miscellaneous provisions in highways cases including highways cases involving snow and ice, a common scenario in relation to highways slipping and tripping claims.

This chapter will also look at common law negligence, and how that may be used for street furniture, tripping and slipping incidents on the highway.

This chapter is designed to give the reader an all-encompassing guide to the remaining elements of slipping and tripping cases and how the law may be applied to such cases where the claimant is not assisted under the section 41 of the Highways Act or under the Occupiers' Liability Act 1957 and how the law may be used to bring a claim in such circumstances where the claim will not sit comfortably in relation to the Occupiers Act or the Highways Act 1980 and the duty under section 41 of the Act.

Street Furniture

Section 41 of the Highways Act 1980 applies solely to the fabric of the highway. Therefore the question arises as to what cause of action is applicable in relation to street furniture or items on the highway.

The answer is to be found in the case of *Matthew Shine by his father and Litigation Friend, Mark Shine –v- Tower Hamlets London Borough*

Council 2006 EWCA Civ 852.

This was an appeal from the decision of His Honour Judge Wulwick in the Romford County Court. Matthew Shine then aged 9 years was passing on a road in Bethnal Green together with his mother. The local authority, the appellants in the case, The London Borough of Tower Hamlets had installed a number of bollards on the footway and the purpose of the bollards and an item of street furniture was to prevent persons parking on the pavement but also to protect pedestrians from the dangers of traffic. The claimant left his mother, went up to one of the bollards and attempted to leap frog it in the ordinary way and unfortunately the bollard was unsecured and had not been properly secured to the floor and under the impact from Matthew it wobbled and he fell off and injured himself.

A claim was advanced under two grounds both under the Highways Act 1980 and as a matter of common law negligence.

It was found in relation to the issue of negligence:

> *"the elements of negligence were on the Judge's findings clearly established. He held as we have seen that it was foreseeable that Matthew or rather a child in Matthew's position would quite likely leap frog one of these bollards.*
>
> *It was also established on the Judge's findings that it was an insecure state and nothing else had caused Matthew's injuries. Was the local authority therefore negligent in the sense of being culpable in not putting the bollard in order at the time they came to know of its insecurity?"*

At paragraph 24 of the Judgment he went on to say:-

> *"True as it is that the witness for the local authority explained that by saying if one left the bollard unattended it might get more dangerous to the extent that it fell over, blocked the highway or injured someone in some way. Nonetheless in the ordinary course of events according*

to the evidence of Ms Hopkins this bollard should have been made secure well before Matthew Shine had the misfortune to encounter it on 18 October 2001.

I therefore hold the requirements of the law of negligence were fulfilled in this case and I do not think, I have to say, looking at the way in which the world works that the local authority would need to have undue fear about that decision extending their liability in unusual or exorbitant ways".

This case therefore clearly deals with the issue of street furniture on highways so this may be for example any bollards, signs, benches or the like, which cause injury on the highway to the claimant, can be dealt with in relation to the issue of negligence, and it is therefore not essential on the case law in relation to such a case, to establish a duty under section 41 of the Highways Act 1980 in such an instance.

Claims In Relation To Snow And Ice On The Highway

Section 150 of the Highways Act 1980 provides

"if an obstruction arises in a highway from accumulation of snow or from the falling down of banks on the side of the highway, or from any other cause, the highway authority shall remove the obstruction.

If a highway authority failed to remove an obstruction which is in their duty under this section to remove, a Magistrates' Court may on a complaint by a person, by order require the authority to remove the obstruction, within such a period (not being less than 24 hours) from the making of the order as the court thinks reasonable having regard to all the circumstances of the case.

In considering whether to make such an order under this, and if so what period to allow for the removal of the obstruction, the court shall have particular regard to:-

The character of the highway to which the complaint relates and the nature and amount of the traffic by which it is ordinarily used.

The nature and extent of the obstruction.

The resources of manpower, vehicles and equipment for the time being available to the highway authority for work on highways and the extent to which those resources are being or need to be, employed elsewhere by the authority for such work.

The foregoing provisions of this section apply to a person liable to maintain the highway by reason of tenure, enclosure or prescription as they apply to a highway authority for that highway, and references in those provisions to a highway authority are to be construed accordingly".

Section 150 of the Highways Act, therefore is a potential route in relation to highways slipping and tripping cases.

However, it should be noted that these claims are particularly difficult in light of the decision in *Goodes –v- East Sussex City Council 2000 1 WLR 1356.*

The case of *Goodes –v- East Sussex City Council 2000,* made it clear that the duty under section 41 of the Highways Act to maintain the fabric of the road in good repair did not encompass a duty to prevent or remove the formation of or accumulation of ice or snow.

The House of Lords found in that case:-

"It might be thought that there should be a liability upon a highway authority in England and Wales for damages in the event of injury occurring for a failure to take sufficient measures to prevent the safety of the highways under the conditions of ice or snow but there is no remedy available at common law and if statute is construed in the way I have preferred there is no remedy under the statue. Attempts to achieve such a result by construction seem to me to involve straining

of the statutory language beyond what it can reasonably bear. If a remedy with a financial consequence which it may involve is desired that is a matter for Parliament".

However, Section 41(1)(a) of the Highways Act 1980 states:-

"In particular a highway authority are under a duty to ensure so far as reasonably practical, that a safe passage along a highway is not endangered by snow or ice".

Therefore, if one is dealing with a case that involves the failure to remove ice or snow from the highway, then a cause of action arises for the claimant under section 41 of the Highways Act 1980.

However, the relevant cases show that it is difficult to convince a court to find breach of duty under the Act. There is no statutory definition of reasonably practical although the burden is almost certainly on the highway authority to prove this. A recent example of a case involving snow or ice on a highway can be found in *Rhiannon Pace –v- Swansea City Council 2007*. In this case it was held that whilst a road traffic accident had been caused by ice on a road the highway authority had a statutory defence under the Highways Act 1980 as it had in place an adequate and proper policy for salting the road and the policy had been implemented at the time in question.

The Judge found:

"the fact that ice had formed does perhaps present some reason for concluding that the salting had not been carried out. But the evidence had to be viewed in a wider context of the evidence as a whole. Having regard to the evidence as a whole and in particular the evidence of Mr Mulcahy and Mr Davies, I find that the presence of ice does not indicate that the road had not been salted in accordance with the Winter maintenance plan and in accordance with Mr Mulcahy's instructions.

In the circumstances I find that there was adequate and proper policy for salting and that policy was implemented on the occasion in question and in those circumstances that the defendant has a defence under section 41(1)(a). In those circumstances the claim must fail".

Therefore, if a claim is to be pursued in relation to an accident caused by ice or snow on the highway, it will be necessary to show that the defendant's Winter maintenance programme was either unreasonable or had not been implemented properly. The claimant will therefore require disclosure of not only the full Winter maintenance programme, but evidence as to how it had been implemented.

The claimant must be careful to read the defendant's highway authority's entire policy and check that it had been implemented in accordance with the policy, this may be for example sending out gritters at certain times in accordance with the weather conditions prevalent at the time.

However the case of *Pace –v- City & County of Swansea* makes it clear that the Courts will not readily impose liability in relation to a highway authority who fails to clear ice or snow and causes of action under the Section 41(1)(a) seem to be difficult.

Nuisance In Relation To Highways Claims

A public authority and statutory undertakers can be liable for public nuisance where they create a danger or permit an unreasonable obstruction on the highway.

For a claim to succeed in nuisance, the claimant does not have to prove breach of a duty of care but the cause of action would require a claimant to prove causation and a foreseeability of harm. It may be argued therefore, that nuisance should always be pleaded as an alternative cause of action in relation to slipping and tripping claims on the highway.

It is therefore clear that there is a common law duty to abate highway nuisance and this is also contained within section 133 and 134 of the Highways Act 1980 which sets out:

"to prevent as far as possible the stopping up or obstruction of:-

The highway for which they are the highway authority; and

Any highway for which they are not the highway authority if in their opinion the stopping up or obstruction of that highway would be prejudicial to the interests of their area.

Without prejudice to the foregoing provisions of this section, it is the duty of the highway authority to prevent any unlawful encroachment on any roadside way comprised in a highway for which they are the highway authority".

However, the case of *Kim Ali –v- Bradford City Metropolitan District Council 2010 EWCA Civ 1282* is relevant in relation to claims brought under section 130 of the Highways Act 1980. The question on appeal was whether the highway authority was liable by way of an action for breach of statutory duty under section 130 of the Highways Act and for a nuisance for an accident suffered by a member of the public on a public footpath as a result of slipping on an accumulation of mud and debris.

The case set out that amongst other things there was a duty to remove things deposited on the highway under section 149 of the Highways Act 1980 and under section 150 the duty to remove soil etc from the highway.

It was submitted in Ali that on the facts, Mrs Ali had a valid cause of action against the highway authority for breach of its duty under section 130 and failed to prevent as far as possible the obstruction of a footpath by mud, vegetation and rubbish which made it dangerous for pedestrians.

The Appeal found:

"the arguments by the highway authority against interpreting section 130 as intending to give rise to a civil action for damages are compelling. For the reasons stated I regard it clear that no such right was intended to be created by section 26 of the 1894 Act from which section 130 of the 1980 Act descends. There is nothing in the language of section 130 to suggest that Parliament intended differently.

As its heading and language indicate, section 130 is concerned with the protection of legal rights for the public at large. The rights in question are the rights of the general public to use the highway. This section is about legal rights of access, it is not about the safety of the condition of the highway. It places no obligation on the highway authority to remove obstructions, and thus there is no justification for the implication of such an obligation, especially since express permission is made about the duty of the highway authority to remove obstructions in section 150. The duty under the section itself is a public law duty and its own statutory method of enforcement and the same is true of section 130. After Goodes, Parliament considered whether the law should be extended to create greater rights of compensation against the highway authority for a person who has slipped on the highway. It extended the law but only to the extent set out in section 41(1)(a) which Mrs Ali does not seek to rely for reasons already explained".

In relation to the claim in nuisance in Ali the Court said as follows:

"Mr Welby submitted that where a highway authority had actual knowledge of a danger deposit on the highway or sufficient time has elapsed that it had the means of acquiring the knowledge by a system of inspection it is regarded to have continued the nuisance and therefore liable to a person who suffers a slipping accident under the principle of establishing Sedleigh Denfield –v- O'Callaghan as expressed by Lord Viscount Maughan at page 894 which said in my opinion an occupier of land which continues a nuisance if with the knowledge or presumed knowledge of its existence he fails to take any reasonable means to bring it to an end though with ample time to do so".

"*However it is said to apply the rule of Sedleigh Denfield to the present case would involve extended rationale to a very different type of situation from what the Court was considering. The legal issue in Sedleigh Denfield concerned the standard of conduct ordinarily required of an occupier of land towards his neighbour --- to compare the relationship between neighbouring private land owners with the relationship between the highway authority and the users of a highway is not to compare like with like*"

The case went on:

"*the highway authority provides a complex statutory code given in the obligations of highway authorities. To require highway authorities to carry out regularly precautionary inspections of public footpaths of all descriptions to see if they are kept free from obstructions would have substantial and uneconomic implications for local authorities. The Courts do not have the tools for carrying out a cost benefit analysis for deciding on the merits of imposing such an obligation analogous to the impact assessment which a department putting forward a pro-posal for legislative change would be required to carry out. Further the current legislation contains specific provisions which regulate the powers and duties of highway authorities with respect of removal of highway obstructions and establishing a method for enforcement of the duty to use sections 149 and 150. That method includes pro-vision for the balancing of risk against resources and individual cases. See section 130(3). It is accepted that Parliament did not intend that breach of highway authority's duty under section 150 for the removal of obstructions should give rise to a private action in damages. In these circumstances, for the Courts to impose such a liability through the law of nuisance would be a blunt instrument, interfere with a carefully regulated statutory scheme and usurp the proper role of Par-liament. I should stress that we are not concerned here with a nuisance which was created by a highway authority. There has never been a suggestion that a highway authority would not be liable in common law negligence for a nuisance which it created*".

It seems from the case of Ali that public authorities are unlikely to be liable for adopting or continuing a nuisance.

It seems that public authorities will be liable in public nuisance where they create a danger or permit an unreasonable obstruction on the highway. An example can be found in *Hale –v- Hant & Dorset Motor Service Limited and another 1947 2ALL ER 628.*

Conclusions

It can therefore be seen from the above causes of action highlighted, in certain circumstances causes of action can be grounded in either negligence, nuisance or relevant statutory provisions of the Highways Act 1980.

When a claim is presented, all of the relevant causes of action should be explored and all of the relevant causes of action should be pleaded, if applicable.

It is unusual for a claim to succeed in nuisance where it is likely to fail in negligence, although that does not mean it is impossible.

Without doubt, the claimant's solicitor should seek advice from counsel given that pleading the correct cause of action will be essential with reference to the facts of the case and it is sometimes the case that there will be more than one potential cause of action in a slipping or tripping claim which occurs on the highway, especially in circumstances where street furniture, snow or ice, or the claim is likely to fall outside of the provisions of section 41 of the Highways Act in the case of a highways slipping and/or tripping claim.

CHAPTER TEN
LITIGATION TIPS & TACTICS IN
SLIPPING AND TRIPPING CASES

One of the ways in which the claimant's lawyer can deal effectively with highways slipping and tripping claims, occupiers' claims and defective premises claims is not only in the quality of the evidence of the case and assessing the same together with the credibility of the witness but the litigation tactics one chooses to pursue in pursuing the claim on behalf of the claimant. Litigation tactics in such cases can be just as effective at settling the case, and will potentially help to achieve a positive outcome on cases which are less evidentially sound using the following methods to encourage settlement in relation to a case.

The following chapter deals with matters in highways slipping and tripping cases, occupiers' liability cases and defective premises act claims and potential tactics one can use in dealing with such cases to progress the case.

Not all tactics will be of use in all cases, but the following sections are intended to give a brief synopsis of how, used appropriately, these tactics can be used against the defendant to encourage and progress cases especially when dealing with cases within a fixed costs regime.

Early Disclosure

Claims under the Highways Act 1980

In almost every highways slipping and tripping case, the claimant will ordinarily wish to have sight of disclosure of the following documents from the local authority:-

- The defendant's highways records including inspection records and maintenance records.

- The defendant's highways repair and intervention policy valid at the date of the accident.

- The defendant's disclosure in relation to similar incidents and/or other slips, trips and falls in the last twelve months and post six months and for the period six months after the accident.

- A copy of the accident report form if available.

- Any CCTV footage.

Indeed if one looks at paragraph 3.7 of the Personal Injury Pre Action Protocol this says as follows *"the defendant's insurers will have a maximum of three months from the date of acknowledgement of the claim to investigate. No later than the end of that period the defendant's insurer shall reply stating whether liability is denied and if so giving reasons for their denial and including any alternative version of events relied upon."*.

In addition, paragraph 3.10 says:

"if the defendant denies liability he should enclose with a letter of reply documents in his possession which are material to the issues between the parties and which should be likely to be ordered to be disclosed by the Court either on an Application for Pre-Action Disclosure or on disclosure on proceedings". Section B of the Pre-Action Protocol provides a list of documents that the defendant will be expected to disclose in relation to a highways tripping claim and these include "documents from highway authority for a period of 12 months prior to the accident:–

- *records of inspection for the relevant stretch of highway;*

- *maintenance records including records of independent contractors working in the relevant area;*

- *records of any minutes of highway authority meetings where maintenance or repair policy has been discussed or decided;*

- *records of complaints about the state of the highway;*

- *records of other accidents which have occurred on the relevant stretch of highway".*

The claimant in a highways case will almost certainly need to see all of these documents from the Highway Authority before a decision can be reached in relation to liability.

One of the historic difficulties with highways cases has been that the defendant gives partial disclosure of the documentation or it drip feeds the documents over a period of time and the claimant has to keep going back and forward to the highway authority asking for disclosure of further documents which were not included as part of the response and there are some insurers that use this tactic time and time again.

One of the solutions to this issue, is for the claimant to include in the CNF all of the documents that the claimant will expect to see under the Personal Injury Pre-Action Protocol if liability is denied and the claim subsequently exits the low value portal and goes into the Pre-Action Protocol for personal injury claims. A copy of the full protocol can be found at:

www.justice.gov.uk/courts/procedure-rules/civil/protocol/pot-_pic#IDACJKCC.

It is advisable, that if the full disclosure is not given once the claim falls out of the portal a further request is sent in writing to the defendant asking again for disclosure of the full documents failing which an application for pre-action disclosure will be made and the costs sought of the application.

If after the end of the protocol period the defendant has still not given full disclosure, a final letter should be sent warning the defendant of the matters set out in the Personal Injury Pre-Action Protocol and again seeking disclosure of the full documents or an application will be issued and the costs sought of the application.

One of the difficulties historically with pre-action disclosure applications for claimants is that where an application for pre-action disclosure is made under CPR 48.12 *"the general rule is that the court will award the person whom the order is sought his costs of the application and of complying with any order made on the application"*.

However, the notes in the White Book at page 1522 48.11 state that *"if however that party has unreasonably opposed the Application or failed to comply with any relevant pre-action protocol the court may well make a different order"*.

Therefore, before any application for pre-action disclosure is made it puts the claimant in a far stronger costs position when it comes to the assessment of costs at the application hearing.

It will be the case that post-Jackson claimant lawyers will want to make early applications for pre-action disclosure so quick decisions can be made on cases as soon as they fall out of the portal and go into fixed costs as to whether cases are to be litigated or not.

Occupiers' Liability Claims Pre-Action Disclosure

On an occupiers' liability case, the claimant will want to see the following documents from the defendant:-

- Photographs of the area where the accident took place and the defect together with any measurements taken.

- The defendant's inspection records, maintenance records, risk assessments and any witness statements.

- The defendant's clean as you go policy if applicable together with training records and cleaning records.

- The defendant's disclosure in relation to similar incidents and other trips, slips or falls in the last twelve months before the accident and six months post-accident.

- A copy of the accident report form.

- A copy of any witness evidence if available, and the defendant's letter of denial with documents in support.

The Personal Injury Pre-Action Protocol does not set out what documents would be required under the protocol in relation to an occupiers' liability case, but these would largely be similar to the documents that would be requested in a highways tripping claim and the reader is referred to the section above in this regard.

However if the claimant suffered an accident in the workplace, i.e. a slipping or tripping claim that was brought under the Occupiers' Liability Act, the pre-action protocol makes it clear that the defendant would be required to disclose the following documents that would be potentially of assistance to the claimant in relation to assessing liability in a claim "workplace claims"

- *Accident book entry.*

- *First aider report.*

- *Surgery report.*

- *Form/supervisor accident report.*

- *Safety representative's accident report.*

- *RIDDOR Reporting of Injuries, Diseases and Dangerous Occurrences Regulations report to HSE.*

- *Other communications between defendants and HSE.*

- *Minutes of health and safety committee meetings where the accident/matter considered.*

- *Reports to the DSS.*

- *Documents listed above relative to any previous accidents/matter identified by the claimant and relied upon as proof of negligence.*

- *Earnings information where defendant is the employer.*

- *Documents produced with the requirements of the Management of Health & Safety at Work 1992 – pre-accident risk assessment required by regulation 3.*

- *Post-accident reassessments required by regulation 3.*

- *Accident investigation reports prepared in implementing the requirements of regulation 4, 6 and 9.*

- *Health surveillance records as appropriate cases required by regulation 5.*

- *Information provided to employers under regulation 8.*

- *Documents related to the health and safety training required by regulation 11".*

In addition, if the claim was brought under the Workplace Health Safety & Welfare Regulations 1992 the defendant would be required to disclose the following documents under the Regulations:-

- Repair and maintenance records required by regulation 5.

- Housekeeping records to comply with the requirements of regulation 9.

- Hazard warning signs or notices to comply with regulations 17 (traffic routes).

If it involves an occupiers or slipping claim, brought by an employee against an employer during the course of their employment, the relevant regulations can be cited when seeking disclosure from the defendant. Nevertheless, some or all of the above may be useful for a non employee occupiers' slipping and tripping claim for example in a supermarket or the like, and in particular the cleaning records and inspection records will be relevant in such cases.

It is important in relation to occupiers cases, to press the defendant for early disclosure of the above documents as soon as the matter falls out of the low value portal and into fixed costs since it will be very difficult to make a decision on liability for the claimant without the disclosure of the relevant cleaning and inspection records, for example a supermarket case.

Again the defendant should be given an opportunity to disclose the documents on a voluntary basis and given three letters with costs warnings and then an application for pre-action disclosure should be made at the earliest opportunity for specific disclosure pre-action, under CPR 31.16 if the defendant has still not provided all of the relevant disclosure by that point. Again one finds in practice in run of the mill slip and tripping cases, that defendants often drip feed disclosure of documents and it is important therefore that especially when dealing with matters in fixed costs that the defendant discloses all of the relevant documentation needed to assess liability at the earliest opportunity so early decisions can be made for claimant lawyers on fixed costs cases as soon as the matter exits the low value portal.

Defective Premises Act 1972 Disclosure

In such a case, it will be important for the claimant to have early disclosure of the following documents:-

- A copy of the full Lease and plan of the property to show the area demised by the Lease.

- Photographs of the area where the accident took place and the defect with measurements if possible.

- The defendant's inspection of maintenance records, risk assessment and any witness statements.

- The defendant's disclosure in relation to similar incidents and other slips, trips or falls in the last twelve months before the accident and six months post-accident.

- Accident report forms.

- Witness evidence if available.

- Any CCTV footage.

Again, it may be argued that in relation to such matters the same rules are likely to apply and when bringing a defective premises claim against the Landlord (see separate chapter on defective premises claims), it will be particularly important to have early disclosure of documents in relation to the inspection and maintenance of the property in order to assess liability and it will be difficult for the claimant's lawyer to assess the case without early disclosure of the documentation.

Again, relevant Pre-Action Disclosure Applications should be made where necessary.

Witness Statements

It is arguable that the witness statement is the most important document in the whole case in relation to a highways slipping and tripping case, an occupiers' liability case or a Defective Premises Act 1972 case.

The witness statement of the claimant and all the witnesses must be detailed especially with regards to the mechanism of the accident and causation.

As a general guide, the witness statement should contain all the relevant detail from the moment the claimant left the property, to the moment that the claimant returned again including details as to how the injury was sustained and all the losses that flowed as a result of the injury.

One sometimes sees witness statements in such cases which are lacking in detail and in particular detail as to the mechanism of the fall or even the size of the defect or the measurements.

The witness statement in such a case should exhibit all the relevant exhibits to the witness statement including photographs of the defect with measurements including detailed explanations as to who took the photographs, when they were taken and the circumstances in which the photographs were taken.

As a general rule, in a highways slipping and tripping case or a slip and trip case in a supermarket which are the common cases which one comes across in practice, the following information should be included in detail in the witness statement:-

- The date of the accident.

- The time of the accident.

- The exact location of the accident.

- The layout of the road or locus where the accident took place.

- The direction in which the claimant was walking.

- Where the claimant was going from and to at the time of the accident.

- Details of any witnesses to the accident.

- Whether the claimant had consumed alcohol or not.

- Whether the claimant was carrying anything.

- The type of footwear that the claimant was wearing.

- The weather conditions at the time of the accident.

- Whether the claimant was carrying anything that could have contributed to the slip, trip or fall.

- Whether there were any other factors that could have contributed to the slip, trip or fall.

- The exact measurements of the defect or matter that caused the claimant to slip, trip or fall including the width, depth and height.

- Whether the claimant has seen the defect or the material that caused the trip or fall, prior to the fall.

- If the claimant is aware of any other similar complaints or accidents prior to the accident and if so how these matters came into the claimant's knowledge exhibiting documents in support of that assertion.

- Whether the claimant has seen the defect before and if so, when.

- How the claimant fell or tripped or slipped?

- Did the claimant slip or trip on their left foot or their right foot or both?

- What part of the claimant's foot got caught in the hole and at what point did the claimant's foot get caught in the hole?

- In which direction did the claimant fall and on what part of the body did the claimant land?

- What happened after the accident?

- Did anyone attend to the claimant immediately after the accident?

Those are just some of the examples one can ask when preparing a proof of evidence for a claimant and if it provides some example as to the types of questions one would ask when taking a proof of evidence from a claimant in relation to a slip, trip or a fall accident.

The claimant's witness statement is the most important document in the whole case and the document upon which the claimant will primarily be cross examined at the trial in relation to the issues of liability and breach of duty. It is also important to stress that the statement should be in the claimant's own words. It does not assist the court where the statement looks like it has been drafted by the claimant's lawyer.

It is therefore important that the claimant's statement has sufficient detail in order to achieve this outcome.

Photographs

When dealing with any slip or trip case, particularly for a defect in the highway or a defect on private land, it is essential that after the accident the claimant is advised to go and take clear colour photographs of the defect with measurements with a ruler if possible and the photographs are signed and dated by the claimant.

It is also very helpful if the claimant can place an arrow next to the defect showing the direction of travel at the point of impact, and the claimant should also be asked to mark the photographs to confirm the exact point that the claimant tripped over within the defect.

If the claimant does not have a ruler or other measuring implement available, sometimes objects such as keys, coins etc can be placed into the hole and photographs taken to show the depth of the hole at the point that the claimant tripped or fell over it.

Good clear colour photographs are essential in relation to these types of claims and it is essential that the claimant is advised to take early photographs as soon as the accident happened.

One may sometimes wish to consider using an independent professional company to take such photographs given their importance to the case.

If photographs are provided by a third party they should be attached and exhibited to a witness statement explaining the dates that the photographs were taken, who took them and the position or occupation of the person taking the photographs.

If the claimant took the photographs then these should be exhibited in the claimant's witness statement explaining who took the photographs, when they were taken and what they show.

Sketch Plans/Plans of the Locus

It is always helpful in highways slipping and tripping cases and occupiers' cases on private land, to have a plan of the locus, and the claimant should be asked to mark on the plan exactly where the accident occurred at an early stage in the case, together with the direction of travel at the point of the slip, trip or fall.

This not only aids the investigation of the case for the defendant in that they can locate the defect quickly on local authority plans or in relation to the occupiers' plans, but it enables the claimant early on to have a contemporaneous record of how the accident occurred and the manner in which it occurred.

A clear sketch plan together with the photographs of the defect and of the locus will enable the matter to proceed much more quickly and so all parties to the action can be sure that they are working on the correct defect at the relevant locus. In some highways claims there can often be a number of defects in the highway or on the pavement at the same location and where there are a number of defects it is essential for the claimant to identify which one was the subject of the trip, slip or fall claim.

Further, in relation to highways cases, if the road is in a general poor state of disrepair and there are a number of defects on the road often a video taken on a mobile phone or clear colour images of the locus can enable the claimant to build a case that the road generally at that location was in a poor state of disrepair. This is discussed in more detail in the Highways Act claim chapter and the reader is referred to this section for more information.

Part 18 Questions

Finally, part 18 questions can also be a useful tool in relation to highways slipping and tripping claims, defective premises claims and occupiers' liability act claims.

Part 18 questions are used relatively sparingly by claimant lawyers when pursuing claims against occupiers, highway authorities and landlords under defective premises claims. They can however be a useful tool to press the defendant for information in relation to cleaning and inspection cases in supermarket slipping and tripping cases, inspection regimes in relation to highways cases and maintenance records in relation to Defective Premises Act claims.

The use of part 18 questions will of course turn on the merits of the case and the facts of the case but they are mentioned here as a useful tool that the claimant's solicitor can employ if the defendant is delaying providing information that is sought and is key to the issue of liability.

Summary

In short, in a post-Jackson era, it will be essential for defendant's insurers to give early disclosure in relation to all types of slipping, tripping and defective premises claims.

Claimant lawyers will need to make early decisions on these cases in relation to the issue of liability and these aims cannot be achieved unless the defendant gives early and frank disclosure to assess systems of inspection, maintenance and the like in relation to section 58 defences under the highways claims, and inspection regimes for example in supermarket slipping and tripping cases pursuant to *Ward –v- Tesco*.

The claimant's lawyer, it may be argued in a fixed costs regime, should always have pre-action disclosure at the forefront of his mind when making decisions as to liability and having all the relevant disclosure to hand before making decisions on liability.

Putting the defendant on early notice as soon as the case exits the low value portal that an application will likely be made in the event of non-compliance will enable the claimant's employer to protect the costs position should it be necessary to issue such an application.

CHAPTER ELEVEN
DEFECTIVE PREMISES ACT 1972 AND CLAIMS UNDER THE LANDLORD AND TENANT ACT 1985 – UPDATED WITH NEW CASES

The Defective Premises Act 1972 represents an important piece of legislation when dealing with slipping and tripping claims that may occur on a landlord's premises.

Claimant lawyers in practice, will find that the Act is particularly useful in dealing with claims where it is likely to be difficult establishing liability under the Occupiers' Liability Act 1957 because the landlord is not the occupier of the property.

It is an important cause of action because any claimant who is injured in the landlord's property can bring an action under the Defective Premises Act 1972 and it is not just limited to tenants of the property.

The Duty of Care Under the Act

The duty of care is set out in Section 4 of the Act which says as follows:-

> *"Where premises are let under a tenancy which puts on the landlord an obligation to the tenant for the maintenance or repair of the premises, the landlord owes a duty to all persons who might be reasonably expected to be affected by the defect and the state of the premises a duty to take care as is reasonable in all the circumstances to see that they are reasonably safe from personal injury or from damage to their property caused by the relevant defect.*
>
> *The said duty is owed if the landlord knows (whether as a result of being notified by the tenant or otherwise) or if he ought to have*

known in all the circumstances of the relevant defect.

In this section relevant defect means a defect in the state of the premises existing at or after the material time or arising from, or continuing because of, an act or omission by the landlord which constitutes or would if he had been on notice of the defect, constituted a failure by him to carry out his obligation to the tenant for the maintenance or repair of the premises and for the purpose of the foregoing provision at the material times means:-

> *When the tenancy commenced before the act, the commencement of the act; and*
>
> *In all other cases, the earliest of the following times that is to say –*
>
> *i) The time that the tenancy commences.*
>
> *ii) The time when the tenancy agreement is entered into.*
>
> *iii) The time when possession is taken of the premises in contemplation of the letting"*

It goes on to say at subsection 4:-

> *"Where premises are let under a tenancy which expressly or impliedly gives the landlord the right to enter into the premises to carry out any description of maintenance or repair of the premises, then, as from the time he first is, or by notice or otherwise can put himself, in a position to exercise the right and so long as he does or can put himself in that position, he shall be treated for the purpose of subsection 1 – 3 but for no other purpose, as if he were under an obligation to the tenant for the description or maintenance of the repair of the premises, but the landlord shall not owe the tenant any duty by virtue of the subsection in respect of any defect in the state of the premises arising from, or continuing because of, a failure to carry out an annex obligation expressly imposed by the tenancy".*

The Relevant Defect

Within the meaning of the Act, the relevant defect is likely to mean a defect that arises from or continues because of an act or omission by the landlord. In the context of slipping and tripping claims this is likely to mean such defects as leaking water pipes. Often cases have involved broken bannisters on stairways which have caused falls down the stairway, carpet or flooring which has not been attached to the floor properly which has caused tripping incidents etc.

In relation to any case brought under the Act, it will be necessary firstly for the claimant solicitor to obtain a copy of the Lease, to see if the landlord has a repairing obligation under the tenancy. Under normal circumstances the landlord will have the repair obligation, but it will be necessary to check in the Lease. It is noteworthy, that the landlord is not under any duty under the Act in respect of any defect in the premises which arises from or continues because of a failure to carry out an obligation which the tenancy expressly opposes on the tenant.

This therefore means, that if part of the repair obligation in the property is the tenant's obligation and the tenant has failed to undertake his obligations under the tenancy the landlord would not be liable under the Act.

Therefore it is important for the claimant lawyer to have disclosure of the tenancy agreement at the earliest possible opportunity so the claimant's solicitor can establish exactly what the landlord's repair obligation was under the tenancy.

Is A Landlord An Occupier?

Landlords are not usually occupiers. When a landlord departs control of the property by granting a Lease over it. A landlord will usually be an occupier for any areas not demised by the Lease i.e. common stairways and halls etc.

Therefore if the claimant's solicitor is looking at an accident which has occurred in a common part which more often than not will be common stairways or halls, for example in a block of flats or a shared stairway to a property, it is important to check the Lease to consider which areas are demised by the Lease and which are not.

If a landlord still has control of an area not demised by the Lease such as a common stairway or hall, then the landlord would still be the occupier for the purpose of the Occupiers' Liability Act 1957 and a claim could still be brought by the tenant/claimant within the meaning of the Act.

Tenants As Occupiers

If a claimant has slipped or tripped and is not the tenant within the property, then it will be important for the claimant's solicitor to consider not only a potential claim under the Defective Premises Act 1972 against the landlord, but also a claim against the tenant under the Occupiers' Liability Act 1957.

If a landlord has granted a tenancy, then it is likely that the tenants will be the occupier for the purpose of the 1957 Act and providing that the claimant is a visitor within the meaning of the 1957 Act, in any area demised by the lease, then a claim may be appropriately brought against the tenant under the 1957 Act. It will of course be important in such circumstances to check that the tenant is insured for such a risk or that the tenant has the money to fund any Judgment before such a claim is to be pursued.

Can The Landlord Delegate Liability Under The Defect Premises Act 1972?

Under the Defective Premises Act 1972, the Landlord cannot delegate responsibility under the Act to a letting agent or the like, to carry out the landlord's obligations under the Act.

Whereas the Occupiers Liability Act 1957 has specific provisions in relation to independent contractors and there is a defence under the Occupiers' Liability Act 1957 where the occupier has employed an independent contractor, no such provisions are drawn into the 1972 Act. It is argued that there is good reason for this, since the Defective Premises Act is designed to protect tenants and other visitors to the premises against unscrupulous landlords who do not carry out their repair obligations properly within the meaning of the Act.

To allow a landlord to delegate such obligations to a letting agent or the like, would frustrate the intention of the Act. It is therefore argued that if a landlord has delegated his responsibilities under the 1972 Act to a letting agent or the like and the letting agent has failed in their obligations under the Act, then the landlord's remedy is to sue the letting agent for breach of contract. The Claimant clearly would have no such cause of action, since they would not be privy to the contract between the letting agent and the landlord. In such circumstances, and one often sees these types of defences in practice given that many landlords now use letting agents to carry out their obligations to tenants, the defendant should be advised that their correct cause of action if the matter is to be pursued, is to bring in the letting agent as a part 20 defendant or for indemnity or contribution, but the landlord, will still be primarily liable under the 1972 Act, providing that the claimant can satisfy the conditions of section 4 of the Act.

Notice Of The Relevant Defect

A useful case for any Practitioner dealing with a Defective Premises Act case is *Patrick Joseph Hannon –v- Hillingdon Homes Limited 2012*. The claim arose out of an injury to Mr Hannon who suffered when he fell whilst carrying out maintenance work to the central heating and hot water boiler at a house owned by the defendant on 18 February 2008.

The claimant brought his claim in negligence and under the Defective Premises Act 1972. The defendant's main defence to the claim was that it was not negligent and it had a defence to the claim under the

Defective Premises Act 1972. The defendant was therefore required to look at the following issues when considering whether there was a claim under the Act:-

- Were the bannisters part of the furniture?

- Was their failure to replace the bannisters a relevant defect?

- Was the defendant liable to the claimant given that the tenant removed the bannisters?

- Did the defendant have notice of the defect?

The court found in summary that there was a relevant defect in the house that caused the injury to the claimant, it made no difference to the existence of liability that the tenant caused the relevant state of disrepair in the premises. The important issue decided in this case was whether the defendant had notice of the defect.

The defendant in this case argues as follows:-

> *"It was a precondition of Hillingdon's liability under the Defective Premises Act that it had been given notice by the tenant by a notice complied with under the terms of a Lease namely a report which had been given immediately to us as our agent, since it was a defect in the property which was likely to affect public health or stability of the structure. Alternatively it was within the requirement of other faults or disrepair that it had to be reported as soon as possible. He also contended that Hillingdon had never been given notice at best the employers of independent contractors had become aware of the defect when making any of the maintenance visits to the property. That however did not constitute knowledge acquired by Hillingdon".*

The claimant argued against this as follows:-

> *"(a) The notice envisaged by clause 5.10 of the Lease including a*

report to our agents. Any employers including a self-employed employee, of a contractor visiting the property for maintenance and repair purposes that were being undertaken by the landlords clearly such an agent for the purpose of receiving a report of the state of repair of the structure. There have been innumerable such visits over the years, any one of which gave rise to a report since the absence of the bannisters were obvious to all who visited the property.

(b) The notice did not have to be in writing. The tenant by giving access to the house to the maintenance engineer or similar invite he was giving him notice of absence of the bannisters. It followed that the tenant or on innumerable occasions giving Hillingdon notice of the defect.

(c) In any event it was clear that a direct employee for Hillingdon had on occasions, visited the property the most recent of each visit having occurred a few days before Mr Hannon had himself visited. Each visit clearly involved notice being given to Hillingdon.

(d) Hillingdon must have undertaken a number of inspections of the interior of the property as their Landlord in order to ensure that there were no relevant defects that required it to act in order to comply with the remedial and maintenance obligations under the Lease. There was no such evidence that such visits had occurred and if that was so, that absence of inspection visits was itself a breach by Hillingdon as Hillingdon's repair obligations gave rise to an obligation to repair such disrepairs as would have been observed had an inspection visit occurred."

The Court found:

"Finally, in any event section 44 of the DPA gave rise to a liability whereas in this case the Landlord had an express right to enter the property to carry out repairs and a further express right to visit and inspect the property for the purpose of seeing whether it could exercise that right. That right arose even if Hillingdon had not in fact exercised its right to repair and inspect since the DPA liability arose

> *"from the time when the notice or otherwise it could have put itself in a position to exercise" the right to inspect and carry out the repairs. Since Hillingdon could have inspected and repaired the bannister and could have done so at any time over the period of the tenancy, it was liable for not carrying out those repairs even if it did not have notice of the defect. For all of those reasons Hillingdon have been given sufficient and appropriate notice even if, which was not the case, it was necessary for that notice to have been given in order to have found liability under the DPA".*

It can therefore be seen from the case of *Hannon –v- Hillingdon*, that this is an important case in relation to whether actual notice of the defect is required under the Act for the landlord to be liable. To succeed under the Act, the defendant must either therefore have actual or constructive knowledge of the defect under section 4 (2) or imputed knowledge under section 4 (4) of the Defective Premises Act 1972.

Thus under section 4 (4) of the Act, the defendant will be under a duty if he had the right or obligation to enter that part of the premises to repair the defect in question. If the defendant did have the right he is under a duty in respect of that defect not withstanding that he either knew about it nor could reasonably have known. He is treated for the purpose of the Act as if he were under a duty imposed in respect of the defect he knew or should have known about. Knowledge of the defect is thus in effect implied against the landlord.

Practitioners will note that the majority of tenancy agreements contain the provision for the landlord to enter the premises to carry out the repairs, although this should be checked and a copy of the Lease should be requested.

This also sits squarely with the case of *Sykes –v- Harry 2001 EWCA Civ 167* where the Court said:

> *"it was not necessary to prove that the landlord had notice, actual or constructive, of the defect which gave rise to the risk of injury".*

The court went on to say that this was because *"because the relevant defect is also defined in terms of the landlord's failure to carry out such obligations, and thus the argument might otherwise arise as to whether or not he had notice of the relevant defect, the relevant defect is defined in terms which precludes such arguments"*.

In order to establish breach of duty against the landlord, the claimant will still have to show that there was a relevant defect in the premises, and that there was a foreseeable risk of injury in order for the claim to succeed.

Therefore, the claimant will also have to show on balance, that the landlord had the repairing obligation for the property and the right to enter the property for maintenance and repairs under the Lease.

Defective premises claims can be incredibly technical and counsel's advice should always be sought where there is doubt over any provisions of the Act.

The Landlord & Tenant Act 1985

A chapter on landlords' liability would not be complete without a mention of the Landlord & Tenant Act 1995.

Section 11(1) of the Landlord & Tenant Act 1985 sets out as follows:-

"In a Lease to which this section applies, as to which see sections 13 and 14, there is an implied covenant by the Lessor:–

To keep in repair the structure and exterior of the dwelling house (including drains, gutters and external pipes.

To keep in repair and proper order the installations in the dwelling house for the supply of water, gas and electricity and for sanitation (including basins, sinks, baths and sanitary conveniences, but not other fixtures, fittings and appliances for making use the supply of water, gas and electricity).

To keep in repair and proper working order the installations in the dwelling house for space, heating and heating water".

Morgan –v- Liverpool Corporation 1927 2KB 131 held that for a section 11 implied covenant to ground an action against the landlord, the landlord must have notice of the defect to be remedied.

It is clear that only a tenant could bring an action in damages for injury under the legislation, since other visitors to the property would not have privity of contract to sue under the Lease. An action under the Landlord and Tenant Act 1985 thus presents the claimant with another potential avenue for damages in the event of the tenant being injured in the property and where there are difficulties with any claim under the Defective Premises Act 1972.

Summary & Conclusions

It therefore seems that claims brought against landlords under the Defective Premises Act or for tenants under the Landlord & Tenant Act 1985 are extremely difficult for landlords to defend. This is primarily because as in the case of the Defective Premises Act 1972, actual notice of the defect will not be required in order for the claimant to succeed in a claim under the Act, subject to the provisions set out above.

This is why it is submitted that claims under the Defective Premises Act made against landlords are often successful providing that the claimant can show that there was a relevant defect, the defendant had the repair obligation, and a right to enter the property for maintenance or repairs.

When considering any action under the Defective Premises Act 1972 or the Landlord and Tenant Act 1985 it is always helpful for the claimant to seek disclosure from the defendant of the following documents:-

- A copy of the Lease.

- A copy of any previous accidents or injuries at the property for other tenants.

- The history and maintenance of the repairs to the property and what steps were taken to repair the property.

- In the case of local housing associations especially, whether there was any regular maintenance or visits to the property.

It is clear that in many cases the landlord attempts to blame a letting agent or the like, will not be a successful defence to a claim under the Act, since the duty under the 1974 Act cannot be delegated to third parties hence the landlord will be liable subject to the provisions set out above.

UPDATE 2018: Defective Premises Act Cases

GILLIAN DRYSDALE v JOANNE HEDGES (2012) - A landlord owed no duty of care under the 1972 Act. The Judgment set out as follows:-

Breach of the duty in contract and/or under Section 4 of the Defective Premises Act 1972

The terms of the tenancy agreement

78. *The premises demised was "All those premises known as 3 Canning Street...".*

79. *Clauses 2.1-2.11 made provision for the tenant's responsibility for the interior of the premises, fixtures and fittings, appliances and like matters. Clause 2.11 granted the landlord access on notice to enter the premises to inspect the state of repair and decoration thereof "and to paint the outside of the Premises or Building and generally*

to carry out therein or therefrom any repairs, additions, alterations or other works which may appear to the Landlady...to be necessary to the Premises or Under the heading "Cleaning" Clauses 2.15 -2.17 dealt with chimneys, the insides of windows and smoke alarms. By Clause 2.18 the tenant was not to cause or allow obstructions/blockages concerning internal plumbing, drains down-pipes and gutters.

By Clause 2.32 the tenant covenanted not to carry out any decoration to the Premises without prior consent and not to "alter nor interfere with the construction or arrangement of the Premises" without consent.

80. *The Landlord's covenants were contained in Clause 3 the relevant subclause of which is 3.2 whereby the landlord covenanted:*

"3.2 To provide and maintain the structure and exterior...in good repair.....except in respect of damage caused by the Tenant or any invitee or insofar as the Tenant is liable to keep the Premises in repair under clause 2 of this agreement."

Section 4 of the Defective Premises Act 1972

81. This provides:

"Landlord's duty of care in virtue of obligation or right to repair premises demised.

(1) Where premises are let under a tenancy which puts on the landlord an obligation to the tenant for the maintenance or repair of the premises, the landlord owes to all persons who might reasonably be expected to be affected by defects in the state of the premises a duty to take such care as is reasonable in all the circumstances to see that they are reasonably safe from personal injury or from damage to their property caused by a relevant defect.

(2) The said duty is owed if the landlord knows (whether as the result of being notified by the tenant or otherwise) or if he ought in all the circumstances to have known of the relevant defect.

(3) In this section "relevant defect" means a defect in the state of the premises existing at or after the material time and arising from, or continuing because of, an act or omission by the landlord which constitutes or would if he had had notice of the defect, have constituted a failure by him to carry out his obligation to the tenant for the maintenance or repair of the premises; and for the purposes of the foregoing provision "the material time" means—

(a) where the tenancy commenced before this Act, the commencement of this Act; and

(b) in all other cases, the earliest of the following times, that is to say —
(i) the time when the tenancy commences;
(ii) the time when the tenancy agreement is entered into;
(iii)the time when possession is taken of the premises in contemplation of the letting.

(4) Where premises are let under a tenancy which expressly or impliedly gives the landlord the right to enter the premises to carry out any description of maintenance or repair of the premises, then, as from the time when he first is, or by notice or otherwise can put himself, in a position to exercise the right and so long as he is or can put himself in that position, he shall be treated for the purposes of subsection (1) to (3) above (but for no other purpose) as if he were under an obligation to the tenant for that description of maintenance or repair of the premises; but the landlord shall not owe the tenant any duty by virtue of this subsection in respect of any defect in the state of the premises arising from, or continuing because of, a failure to carry out an obligation expressly imposed on the tenant by the tenancy.

(5) For the purposes of this section obligations imposed or rights given by any enactment in virtue of a tenancy shall be treated as imposed or given by the tenancy.

(6) This section applies to a right of occupation given by contract or any enactment and not amounting to a tenancy as if the right were a tenancy, and "tenancy" and cognate expressions shall be construed accordingly."

I have highlighted what I consider to be the relevant parts of the section.

In order to show a breach of Clause 3.2 and/or Section 4 the Claimant has to show the premises were "not in good repair". *On the meaning of "repair" Mr Fetto drew my attention to* **Quick v Taff Ely Borough Council [1986] QB 809** *where Lawton LJ at p 821 stated :*

"that which requires repair is in a condition worse than it was at some earlier time".

In the same case Dillon LJ cited with approval the earlier words of Atkin LJ in Anstruther-Gough-Calthorpe v Mc Oscar [1924] 1 KB 716 at p 734 that repair "constitutes the idea of making good damage so as to leave the subject so far as possible as though it had not been damaged".

82. *In Alker v Collingwood [2007] 1 WLR 2230 the Court of Appeal had to consider whether a landlord was liable under Section 4 of the 1972 Act for injuries caused to a tenant whose arm went through a glass panel in her front door. The panel was made of ordinary not safety glass. Breach of duty at common law had been abandoned below and the court was concerned essentially with whether or not the unstrengthened glass was "a relevant defect" for the purposes of the 1972 Act. The Claimant's case was that there was a relevant defect because it was dangerous. The Defendant's case was that the glass did not require repair.*

83. *Laws LJ, with whom Carnwath LJ agreed, stated **a duty to repair could not be equated with a duty to make safe and that a duty to keep "in good condition" could not encompass a duty to put in a safe condition**. He added this at p 2236 :*

   "A house may offer many hazards : a very steep stairway with no railings ; a hidden step ; some other hazard inside or outside the house of the kind often found perhaps in particular older properties. I do not think it can be said that the Act requires a landlord on proof only of the conditions I have described for the application of Section 4 to make safe any such dangerous feature."

   His approach echoes that of Lawton LJ in Quick who said at p821:

   "..a tenant must take the house as he finds it; neither a landlord nor a tenant is bound to provide the other with a better house than there was to start with".

84. *As regards the unguarded drop Mr Fetto accepts that there is no evidence that the wall at the time of the accident was any different from when the Defendant acquired the property. It cannot be said that it was out of repair.*

85. *As regards the steps Mr Fetto says this. The stone steps unpainted were in good repair. Painted they became less slip resistant and more prone to become slippery when wet or contaminated. Therefore they required repair. He accepts that context is important but submits that the function of the steps was to provide safe access and that that function was undermined when the steps became slippery because of the paint. He says that the court should bear in mind that those using the steps may be carrying objects of different shapes and sizes, that the steps were not protected against the elements and that they were alongside the unguarded drop.*

86. *This argument is semantically attractive. However, I consider it is stretching the meaning of the word "repair" to apply it to the removal of the paint. The paint did not replace the stone but was additional to it. The stone did not require repair. The paint did not require repair: what it required was removal.*

87. *I would therefore not find on the facts of this case that the presence of the paint caused the steps not to be "in good repair". Accordingly the presence of the paint did not give rise to a breach of Clause 3.2 and Section 4 of the 1972 Act.*

Key Points

1. In order to show a breach of Section 4 the Claimant has to show the premises were "*not in good repair*"

2. *Quick v Taff Ely Borough Council* [1986] QB 809 where Lawton LJ at p 821 stated: "that which requires repair is in a condition worse than it was at some earlier time".

3. A duty to repair could not be equated with a duty to make safe and that a duty to keep "in good condition" could not encompass a duty to put in a safe condition.

CHAPTER TWELVE
CONCLUSIONS AND UPDATE
ON FIXED COSTS FROM THE
JACKSON REPORT 2017

The Future Of Slipping & Tripping Litigation and the Jackson Report 2017

As the reader will have noted from this book, slipping and tripping lit-igation, although sometimes on its facts may appear to be fairly straightforward, one can see that how the case law and statute have evolved, and that this is an area of law which is extremely complicated.

From a claimant's solicitors' perspective, the positive about slipping and tripping litigation is that in some instances the case does not always come down simply to the credibility of the claimant, but one can often look especially in occupiers cases and highways cases as to whether the system of inspection was reasonable.

One always has to be aware, that you are going to need a relatively credible client who will succeed on breach of duty and causation in order to pursue a claim either under the Occupiers' Liability Act or the Highways Act and to most extent the Defective Premises Act 1972. However, the lawyers' job becomes much more important in chal-lenging and making the relevant challenges to any section 58 defence or establishing breach under the Occupiers Act or the Defective Premises Act 1972.

These can be highly technical cases with a lot of evidential concerns and that this book in some way will assist the reader to go about addressing the evidential requirements of these cases and what it takes to succeed for the claimant in these types of cases.

It could be argued that even with the inception of the low value portals for slipping and tripping cases in relation to public liability cases and occupiers' liability cases, it is unlikely that the number of these cases will decrease. The claimant's lawyer has to bear in mind that these cases often result in serious injuries, with serious consequences for the claimants involved in this type of litigation and the claimants on these cases deserve access to justice.

It is with some comfort, even with the advent of fixed costs, the costs in the portal and for those claims which fall outside of the portal into fixed recoverable costs, the costs the claimant lawyer can recover for undertaking this type of work are reasonable.

The danger, as with the low value road traffic portals, is that the insurance industry seek to reduce the costs even further to an extent that it is no longer economical for claimant's solicitors to undertake this type of work thus denying access to justice for the victims of these types of accidents which often can involve broken limbs with significant periods of time off work.

It is neither fair nor reasonable for claimants to have to bring these types of cases themselves in the small claims track courts or otherwise, given the often complexities of the law and evidence involved in slipping and tripping litigation, as set out in this book. It may be argued that without the need for a lawyer it would be very difficult for the majority of claimants to bring all but the most straightforward of cases where liability is admitted and even then this presents many difficulties for the claimant.

The need for claimant lawyers in slipping and tripping litigation is great and the costs that the claimant lawyers should be able to recover for undertaking that type of work should be reasonable and proportionate with reference to the complex law that is involved in these types of cases and evidence required to overcome the balance of probability test and establish breach of duty.

The key for claimant lawyers in conducting these cases post-Jackson, is establishing the winners and the losing cases at the very earliest opportunity and obtaining early disclosure from the defendant and full disclosure from the defendant.

It seems likely that the majority of these cases will fall outside of the low value portals and be dealt with within fixed costs. It seems likely that the insurers may for tactical reasons seek to admit some of these claims in the portal even where they have concerns over breach of duty or causation. However, given that the majority of the injuries in these cases tend to be of more than a very low value and tend to be moderate injuries with moderate claims for loss of earnings, care and the like, it is unlikely that the insurers will continue to undertake this tactic, albeit for the very lowest value of claims.

It has to be said, that the claimant lawyers who undertake this type of work for claimants offer real value to claimants, who through other means would not be able to bring their cases.

It is hoped and anticipated that this book assists the claimant lawyers in their way through what can be a very complex set of statutes in relation to slipping and tripping cases.

There are other special considerations which have not been considered as part of this book, for example accidents and slips and trips in the work place which are outside the scope of this work.

If there is any doubt as to liability or causation, in relation to any claims under the Occupiers' Liability Act, the Highways Act, the Defective Premises Act, nuisance or the other statutes referred to in this book, it is always advisable to seek counsel's advice at the earliest opportunity in relation to breach of duty and causation and the relevant causes of action if unsure.

The consequences of failing to plead the correct cause of action can be severe for the claimant.

UPDATE 2018: Further Fix Costs in EL/PL Claims and Mitigating the Effects

The Jackson 2017 supplemental report sets out:-

*"1.4 The proposed Online Solutions Court. Lord Justice Briggs has recommended the creation of an Online Solutions Court, which will deal with cases up to a value of £25,000. **Personal injury, clinical negligence, possession, intellectual property and housing disrepair claims will be excluded from the Online Solutions Court**: see Briggs LJ's Final Report, paragraphs 6.95-6.102.1 It therefore follows that the Online Solutions Court will scoop up some of the current fast track cases and assign to them strictly limited recoverable costs. But a large rump of the fast track will remain in place under the rules proposed in this chapter".*

Extending fixed recoverable costs across the whole fast track

*3.1 The time has come to finish the task. The time has surely come to complete the introduction of FRC across the fast track, not to keep kicking the issue into the long grass. **There is now a general acceptance that FRC should be extended horizontally across the whole of the fast track.** The Bar Council, the Personal Injury Bar Association and many others accept that principle, although they add caveats and points on the details. The South East Circuit ("SEC") in their written submissions state:*

"The SEC can see that fixed costs on the fast-track (claims of up to £25,000) is probably appropriate and, perhaps, desirable. This is because fast-track claims:

a. Are inherently simpler, otherwise they would have been allocated to the multi-track.

b. Are subject to simpler procedural rules and thus involve less and more predictable work, making the idea of broad-brush fixed costs more just and legitimate amongst stake-holders.

c. Are at greater risk of disproportionate costs given the relatively low value of the claims.

d. Constitute the great majority of non-small claims work. According to Civil Justice Quarterly Statistics, 80% of non-small claims cases are allocated to the fast-track."

I agree with that view and recommend that all recoverable costs in the fast track should be fixed.

3.2 Fast track cases for which we do not yet have FRC. We do not yet have FRC for non- personal injury claims. Also, there are categories of personal injury claims for which FRC are not yet in place. In particular: Holiday sickness claims. These are growing in frequency and are the subject of much discussion in the media.9 Appendix 4 plots claimant costs against damages received in 79 such cases.

9 The Government has recently announced an intention to introduce FRC for holiday sickness claims. I support that proposal, but suggest that it should be implemented as part of a comprehensive FRC regime.

During this review, I would suggest that the FRC for such claims (when pursued individually)10 should be the same as for RTA personal injury cases. Employers' liability disease ("ELD"). In recent years, most ELD cases in the fast track have been claims for noise induced hearing loss ("NIHL"). Other fast track personal injury claims which are excluded from the Protocols for Low Value RTA, ELA and PL Claims.

3.3 NIHL. A working party set up by the Civil Justice Council ("CJC"), whose members include claimant and defendant representatives, has put forward proposals for FRC in respect of NIHL claims which remain in the fast track. This agreement was reached following a mediation. A summary of the NIHL mediated agreement is at Appendix 11. The agreement reached also includes a detailed bespoke procedure for NIHL claims, which is not appended but builds on principles of transparency and early information exchange between the parties. Its key recommendations include new forms of letter of claim and letter of response, with the letter of claim accompanied by an audiogram from an accredited audiologist as objective evidence of the claimant's level of hearing. Post-issue there should be specialist standard directions. Certain types of more complex claim have been excluded but the agreement is believed to cover the vast majority of fast track NIHL claims. The final report is with the CJC for approval and I anticipate that this will soon be published by the CJC.

3.4 Lack of data for non-personal injury cases. Despite the best efforts of the assessors and myself, very little data are available in respect of the costs of non-personal injury fast track cases, apart from non-personal injury RTA claims. By definition, such cases fall outside the costs management regime. So there are no court approved budgets for us to look at. The Bar Council's online survey only included two non-personal injury fast track cases. The Housing Law Practitioners Association ("HLPA") has supplied details of 83 fast track disrepair cases, which the FTWG and I have examined with care. These data give an impression of recoverable costs in recent cases where courts have applied the new proportionality rule. But they do not provide evidence relating to agreed costs at settlement on a sufficient volume of claims to allow any degree of statistical confidence about the average amounts recovered on such cases.

3.5 Does that mean we can never fix costs for non-personal injury fast track cases? No. We should put forward what seem to be reasonable figures for each category of case, having regard to:

(i) the proportionality factors set out in CPR rule 44.3(5);
(ii) such data as are available;
(iii) the experience of the assessors;
(iv) the costs of conducting personal injury cases of comparable complexity.

3.6 London weighting. The current FRC rules in the fast track provide for a 12.5% uplift on fixed costs payable to a party who lives in the London area and instructs a legal representative who practises in the London area: see CPR rule 45.29C(2), rule 45.29F(5) and Multi-party actions in holiday sickness cases should proceed in the multi-track, as now. to the extended FRC regime proposed in this chapter.

3.7 Contractual entitlement to costs. Some contracts contain express provisions governing costs in the event of litigation. Examples of such contracts may be mortgages, guarantees or leases. Often, particularly in the case of mortgages, the Court will not be asked to make any costs order at all as the mortgagee will recover its costs from the pro-ceeds of sale of the property. The CPR expressly provide that a mortgagee is not obliged to apply for a costs order: see CPR rule 44.5 and Practice Direction 44, paragraph 7.1. Such costs can also be recovered by a pleaded claim for a contractual indemnity. Even where the Court is asked to make a costs order under the discretionary power in section 51 of the Senior Courts Act 1981, the effect of CPR rule 44.5 is that in contractual costs cases the Court will make an indemnity costs order, unless the contract expressly provides otherwise. This reflects the substantive law position, as indicated by Gomba Holdings (UK) Ltd v Minories Finance Ltd [1993] Ch 171, Church Commissioners v Ibrahim [1997] EGLR 13 and Chaplair Holdings (UK) Ltd v Kumari [2015] EWCA Civ 798, that the contractual entitlement is free from the restraints imposed by procedural rules on recovery of costs and will be free from the FRC regimes suggested in this report. The court will enforce the contractual right, subject to its equitable power to disallow unreasonable expenses. There is nothing in the rule making powers in respect of the CPR which enable the rules to exclude or override a contractual entitlement. Primary legis-lation would be required to alter that position. Although there has been some discussion of this issue at the seminars, the question whether the present position is satisfactory does not fall within my terms of reference. Wider policy issues are in play, such as what would be the effect on overall mortgage interest rates, if mortgagees could not provide for the contractual recovery of litigation costs. In this report, therefore, I do not address the question of contractual entitlement to costs.

3.8 Such cases remain in the fast track. The fact that one party has a contractual entitlement to costs does not prevent a case proceeding in the fast track. The case will be subject to the case management rules of CPR Part 28. If the party with a contractual entitlement to costs succeeds, then the costs position will be as set out in the preceding paragraph.

4 Noise induced hearing loss

4.1 The mediated agreement. As can be seen from appendix 11, the claimant and defendant representatives on the CJC working group have agreed a prescriptive process for dealing with NIHL claims and an accompanying grid of FRC. In my view, the agreement reached is a reasonable one and I endorse it.

4.2 Costs grid for NIHL claims. The agreed costs grid for NIHL claims, which I endorse, is as follows:

Proposed matrix of FRC for NIHL claims (applies to both claimant and defendant recoverable costs)

Stage:	NIHL claims with value less than £25,000
Pre-issue	£4,000 + £500 per extra defendant (reduced by £1,000 if there is an early admission of liability or by £500 if settled before proceedings drafted)
Post-issue, pre- alloc-ation	£5,650 + £830 uplift per extra defendant
Post-alloc-ation, pre-listing	£7,306 + £1,161 uplift per extra defendant
Post-listing, pre- trial	£9,187 + £1,537 uplift per extra defendant
Trial advocacy fee	Not agreed

In addition to the above, a fee of £1,280 is recoverable for restoring a company to the register.

4.3 Counsel's fees and trial advocacy fees. The CJC working group did not reach full agreement on these matters. I have considered the relevant material and the rival submissions made within the working group. I recommend that counsel's fees and trial advocacy fees in NIHL cases should be the same as those which I propose for 'Band 4' cases in the next section of this chapter. Almost all NIHL claims are low value. So, as set out below, the trial advocacy fee will generally be £1,380.

5 The remainder of the fast track

5.1 Proposed matrix of FRC and paradigm cases. Drawing on the work of the FTWG, I propose that all fast track cases be placed into four bands of complexity, Band 1 being the least complex and Band 4 being the most complex. The following are paradigm cases for each band:

Band 1: RTA non-personal injury claims (popularly known as 'bent metal' claims).
Band 2: RTA personal injury claims.
Band 3: ELA and PL accident claims.
Band 4: ELD claims (non-NIHL) and the most complex fast track claims.

5.2 A fuller list of cases suitable for each band. I propose the following:

Band 1: RTA non-personal injury, defended debt cases.
Band 2: RTA personal injury (within Protocol), holiday sickness claims.
Band 3: RTA personal injury (outside Protocol), ELA, PL, tracked possession claims, housing disrepair, other money claims.
Band 4: ELD claims (other than NIHL), any particularly complex tracked possession claims or housing disrepair claims,

property disputes, professional negligence claims and other claims at the top end of the fast track.

5.3 At the allocation stage, the court must have discretion to move individual claims between those bands having regard to the nature of the individual case. Judges should exercise this discretion sparingly and bearing in mind the proportionality factors set out in CPR rule 44.3(5). Any case of particular complexity does not belong in the fast track at all.

5.4 Recoverable costs. I propose that the recoverable costs for each band be as follows: Table 5.2

Matrix of FRC for fast track claims (applies to both claimant and defendant recoverable costs)

	Complexity Band			
Stage:	1	2	3	4
Pre-issue £1,001–£5,000		£104 + 20% of damages	£988 + 17.5% of damages	£2,250 + 15% of damages + £440 per extra defendant
Pre-issue £5,001–£10,000		£1,144 + 15% of damages over £5,000	£1,929 + 12.5% of damages over £5,000	
Pre-issue £10,001–£25,000	£500	£2,007 + 10% of damages over £10,000	£2,600 + 10% of damages over £10,000	
Post-issue, pre-allocation	£1,850	£1,206 + 20% of damages	£2,735 + 20% of damages	£2,575 + 40% of damages + £660 per extra defendant
Post-allocation, pre-listing	£2,200	£1,955 + 20% of damages	£3,484 + 25% of damages	£5,525 + 40% of damages + £660 per extra defendant

Post-listing, pre-trial	*£3,250*	*£2,761 + 20% of damages*	*£4,451 + 30% of damages*	*£6,800 + 40% of damages + £660 per extra defendant*
Trial advocacy fee11	*a. £500 b. £710 c. £1,070 d. £1,705*	*a. £500 b. £710 c. £1,070 d. £1,705*	*a. £500 b. £710 c. £1,070 d. £1,705*	*a. £1,380 b. £1,380 c. £1,800 d. £2,500*

The figures in all boxes are cumulative, except for the trial advocacy fees shown in the bottom line. The word "damages" is used as shorthand for debt, liquidated sum or other monetary relief. There is obviously some difficulty in applying the above table to claims for, or including, non-monetary relief. The court must, I am afraid assign a value to such relief. I propose that a claim for a declaration or injunction should be treated as the equivalent of a claim for £10,000, with the court having power to vary that figure upwards or downwards.

12 For example, in a housing disrepair claim where the defendant is ordered to carry out repairs with a value of £20,000, the injunction requiring such works should be treated as if it were an award of £20,000.

If the claimant succeeds, the specified percentage applies to the relief recovered. If the defendant succeeds, the specified percentage applies to the claim defeated, as valued in the particulars of claim.

*1.1 How are the figures in the table derived? The figures in **Band 1** are based on an analysis of data from Taylor Rose TTKW13 in which fast track RTA claims, with zero general damages but positive special damages between £10,000 and £25,000 in value, were summarised by the chronological stage of litigation at settlement. The mean amounts of recovered base costs were estimated, and adjusted to take account of efficiency savings from fixed costs. These adjustments were necessary to make the figures comparable with the other fast track fixed cost bands.*

*5.6 The figures in **Bands 2 and** 3 are the existing figures for fast track pre-trial fixed costs in personal injury cases with an uplift of 4% to take account of inflation from July 2013 (when those figures were set) to July 2016. I appreciate that a few of those figures have an earlier origin than 2013, but a policy decision was taken in July 2013 to re-adopt those earlier figures. The figure of 4% is derived from the Services Producer Price Index.*

*5.7 The figures in **Band** 4 are based on an analysis of Taylor Rose TTKW data, recording the claimants' costs agreed in a large volume of fast track ELD claims. The figures have been adjusted to take account of efficiency savings from fixed costs. These cases are of comparable complexity to the heaviest non-personal injury claims in the fast track.*

At the allocation stage, the court must have discretion to move individual claims between those bands having regard to the nature of the individual case. Judges should exercise this discretion sparingly and bearing in mind the proportionality factors set out in CPR rule 44.3(5).

5.13 Interim applications and preliminary issues. The costs of any applications properly made (e.g. because the other party is in default) should be recovered separately. There are fixed costs for such applications under CPR rule 45.29H. I propose that in NIHL and Band 4 cases, the provision in CPR rule 45.29H(1) "one half of the applicable Type A and Type B costs" should be amended to "two thirds of the applicable Type A and Type B costs". The fixed recoverable fee for an interim injunction application should be £750.

5.18 Housing claims. The principal categories of housing claims are:

(a) *Defending claims for possession, including mortgage repossession.*
(b) *Claims for unlawful eviction.*
(c) *Homelessness applications, including County Court appeals.*
(d) ***Claims for breach of repairing obligations.***
(e) *Judicial review in respect of housing law issues.*

The HLPA say that they are particularly concerned about housing disrepair claims because these seldom qualify for legal aid. I understand from one of my assessors, who has experience of managing disrepair cases in the fast track, that the FRC regime proposed above would be satisfactory for most disrepair claims.15 **Most such claims would fit into either Band 3 or Band 4.** *Nevertheless, in certain of the cases cited by the HLPA, the recovered costs are higher than the proposed FRC (even allowing for the fact that the HLPA figures include VAT and disbursements). Possibly these are cases which ought not to have been in the fast track at all or possibly they are exceptional cases where the escape clause might be invoked (as to which see below). It is difficult to say without having the details of individual cases.*

5.21 Fast track procedure. The standard directions in Practice Direction 28 may require modification in Band 4 and NIHL cases. For example, in NIHL cases the mediated agreement envisages a set of directions capable of covering the use of experts in different disciplines to deal separately with issues of liability and quantum: those directions would typically allow for questions to be put to the claimant's quantum expert and for the joint instruction of a liability expert. Band 4 cases may require different modifications, but always within the context of the case remaining in the fast track. This is something that the Rule Committee will need to consider in due course.

5.22 Assessment of costs. In most cases, the assessment of recoverable costs should be a straightforward exercise, not requiring judicial input. **In so far as there is any dispute, the court will assess costs. If the case goes to trial, the judge will summarily assess costs at the end of the hearing. In cases which do not go to trial, there should be a shortened form of detailed assessment, of the kind described in the last sentence of Practice Direction 47, paragraph 5.7, with a provisional assessment fee cap of – say – £500.**

Key Points

1. At the allocation stage, the court must have discretion to move individual claims between those bands having regard to the nature of the individual case. Judges should exercise this discretion sparingly and bearing in mind the proportionality factors set out in CPR rule 44.3(5).

2. Costs of interim applications will remain fixed as per CPR 45.29H. In NIHL and Band 4 cases, the provision in CPR rule 45.29H(1) "one half of the applicable Type A and Type B costs" should be amended to "two thirds of the applicable Type A and Type B costs".

3. Who will decide on the bands and when? The pre-action protocols should be amended to require the parties to endeavour to agree pre-action: (a) the appropriate track for cases and (b) in respect of fast track cases, the appropriate band. Claimants should state their proposals in this regard in the letter of claim. Defendants should do the same in the letter of response. If the case reaches allocation stage, the district judge or master should allocate in the usual way and (for fast track cases) specify the band if that is in dispute. Either party could challenge that decision by an application on paper under CPR rule 3.3(5)- (6). I propose that the unsuccessful party on such an application should incur a costs liability of £150. If the case settles before issue or before allocation, then the band allocation decision should fall to the judge assessing costs if there is disagreement between the parties.

MORE BOOKS BY
LAW BRIEF PUBLISHING

A selection of our other titles available now:

'A Practical Guide to Marketing for Lawyers: 2nd Edition' by Catherine Bailey & Jennet Ingram
'A Practical Guide to Advising Schools on Employment Law' by Jonathan Holden
'Certificates of Lawful Use and Development: A Guide to Making and Determining Applications' by Bob Mc Geady & Meyric Lewis
'A Practical Guide to the Law of Dilapidations' by Mark Shelton
'A Practical Guide to the 2018 Jackson Personal Injury and Costs Reforms' by Andrew Mckie
'A Guide to Consent in Clinical Negligence Post-Montgomery' by Lauren Sutherland QC
'A Practical Guide to Running Housing Disrepair and Cavity Wall Claims: 2nd Edition' by Andrew Mckie & Ian Skeate
'A Practical Guide to the General Data Protection Regulation (GDPR)' by Keith Markham
'A Practical Guide to Digital and Social Media Law for Lawyers' by Sherree Westell
'A Practical Guide to Holiday Sickness Claims, 2nd Edition' by Andrew Mckie & Ian Skeate
'A Practical Guide to Inheritance Act Claims by Adult Children Post-Ilott v Blue Cross' by Sheila Hamilton Macdonald
'A Practical Guide to Elderly Law' by Justin Patten
'Arguments and Tactics for Personal Injury and Clinical Negligence Claims' by Dorian Williams
'A Practical Guide to QOCS and Fundamental Dishonesty' by James Bentley
'A Practical Guide to Drone Law' by Rufus Ballaster, Andrew Firman, Eleanor Clot
'Practical Mediation: A Guide for Mediators, Advocates, Advisers, Lawyers, and Students in Civil, Commercial, Business, Property, Workplace, and Employment Cases' by Jonathan Dingle with John Sephton

'The Law of Driverless Cars: An Introduction' by Alex Glassbrook
'A Practical Guide to Costs in Personal Injury Cases' by Matthew Hoe
'A Practical Guide to Alternative Dispute Resolution in Personal Injury Claims – Getting the Most Out of ADR Post-Jackson' by Peter Causton, Nichola Evans, James Arrowsmith
'A Practical Guide to Personal Injuries in Sport' by Adam Walker & Patricia Leonard
'The No Nonsense Solicitors' Practice: A Guide To Running Your Firm' by Bettina Brueggemann
'Baby Steps: A Guide to Maternity Leave and Maternity Pay' by Leah Waller
'The Queen's Counsel Lawyer's Omnibus: 20 Years of Cartoons from the Times 1993-2013' by Alex Steuart Williams

These books and more are available to order online direct from the publisher at www.lawbriefpublishing.com, where you can also read free sample chapters. For any queries, contact us on 0844 587 2383 or mail@lawbriefpublishing.com.

Our books are also usually in stock at www.amazon.co.uk with free next day delivery for Prime members, and at good legal bookshops such as Hammicks and Wildy & Sons.

We are regularly launching new books in our series of practical day-to-day practitioners' guides. Visit our website and join our free newsletter to be kept informed and to receive special offers, free chapters, etc.

You can also follow us on Twitter at www.twitter.com/lawbriefpub.

Printed in Great Britain
by Amazon

77475798R00122